ORGAN TRANSPLANT

**The Debate
Over
Who, How,
and Why**

Successful organ transplantation is one of the most remarkable advances in the history of medicine.

ORGAN TRANSPLANT

The Debate Over Who, How, and Why

Adam Winters

617.95
WIN

THE ROSEN PUBLISHING GROUP, INC.

ORGAN TRANSPLANT

To ALS, who made this and all other books possible.

Published in 2000 by The Rosen Publishing Group, Inc.
29 East 21st Street, New York, NY 10010

Copyright © 2000 by The Rosen Publishing Group, Inc.

First Edition

All rights reserved. No part of this book may be reproduced in any form without permission in writing from the publisher, except by a reviewer.

Library of Congress Cataloging-in-Publication Data
Winters, Adam, 1951–
    Organ transplant : the debate over who, how, and why / Adam Winters.
        p. cm. — (Focus on science and society)
    Includes bibliographical references and index.
    Summary: Discusses the latest medical advances made in the field of organ transplants, how and to whom the process is done, and the ethical questions transplants raise.
    ISBN 0-8239-3209-5 (lib. bdg.)
    1. Transplantation of organs, tissues, etc.—Social aspects—Juvenile literature. 2. Transplantation of organs, tissues, etc.—Moral and ethical aspects—Juvenile literature. [1. Transplantation of organs, tissues, etc.] I. Title. II. Series.
RD120.76 .W56 2000
174'.25—dc21   00-021863

Manufactured in the United States of America

CONTENTS

Patients are often seriously ill while waiting for an organ transplant.

INTRODUCTION

Organ transplantation is one of the most remarkable success stories in the history of medicine. Until very recently, it was the stuff of fairy tales—imagine taking a heart from one person, putting it into the body of another, and having it save that other person's life! In most cases, transplantation is the only hope for thousands of people suffering from organ failure. Unfortunately, the need for donated organs is much greater than the supply. Right now, over 66,000 Americans are waiting to receive donated hearts, lungs, livers, kidneys, and pancreases. Every sixteen minutes, a new name is added to the list. And every day twelve people die waiting for an organ.

The option of organ transplantation, which has only become common in the last twenty years, is a complicated issue because of the technological and medical advances it depends upon, because of the money involved, and because one donor could save up to seven people's lives.

However, perhaps the most complicated of all is the fact that the professionals involved in the actual process of transplantation are forced to make decisions that affect life and death. Funnily enough, the more answers or solutions that are found, the more questions or concerns are raised—questions such as, Is it right to sell a kidney? Is it right to put a pig's heart into a person? Is it right for a doctor to ask a mother with a dying teenage son if she will sign a consent form so that her son's organs can be transplanted into other dying people?

This book will explore some of these issues—first, by describing the scientific and medical aspects involved, and then by taking a look at the ethical questions these aspects raise. Unlike many other books, the goal of this one isn't to fill your head with answers. Rather, it is to leave you with

Timeline

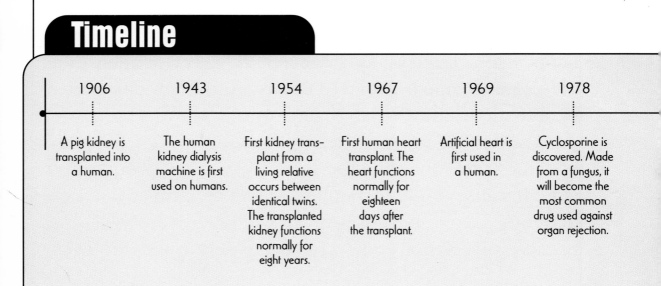

1906	1943	1954	1967	1969	1978
A pig kidney is transplanted into a human.	The human kidney dialysis machine is first used on humans.	First kidney transplant from a living relative occurs between identical twins. The transplanted kidney functions normally for eight years.	First human heart transplant. The heart functions normally for eighteen days after the transplant.	Artificial heart is first used in a human.	Cyclosporine is discovered. Made from a fungus, it will become the most common drug used against organ rejection.

questions—questions that will lead you to think, to talk with your friends, family, and teachers, and maybe even to become an organ donor yourself.

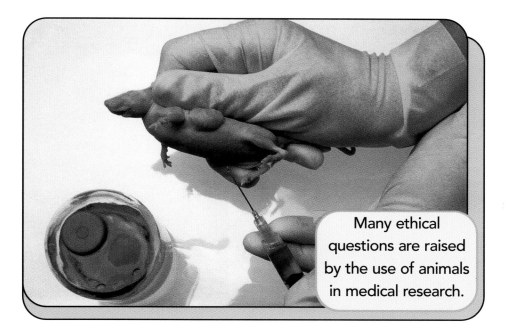

Many ethical questions are raised by the use of animals in medical research.

1982	1983	1984	1986	1989	1996
Barney Clark receives the first artificial heart. He dies 112 days after the transplant.	The first successful single-lung transplant takes place.	Baby Faye becomes the first baboon-to-human heart transplant recipient. She dies twenty days after her xenotransplant.	First successful double-lung transplant. Success rate of pancreas transplants is now 90 percent.	First successful liver transplant from a living relative takes place.	First court-ordered liver transplant occurs. The patient's parents had refused treatment for religious reasons.

CHAPTER 1

TRANSPLANTATION— FROM BEGINNING TO END

There are many illnesses that might lead a person to need an organ transplant. When the illness becomes serious enough that an organ no longer works properly, a doctor may recommend transplant surgery.

Assessment

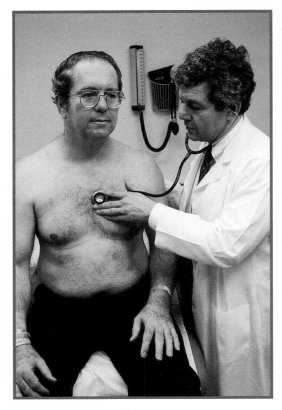

Once you, your family, and your doctor have decided upon transplantation as a solution to your condition, your doctor sends information about you to specialized doctors at a transplant center. These doctors assess you and then put your name on the national waiting list for transplants. This is done through a series of interviews, physical examinations, and medical tests.

On the Waiting List

The amount of time you have to wait depends on the type of transplant you need, the seriousness of your condition, and the availability of donor organs. Some patients wait a few weeks; others must wait a few years.

The Call

When the call comes, you've got to get to your transplant center as fast as possible. (Although if you're very sick, you might already be hospitalized.) Organs don't sit around waiting. And the fresher they are, the better. With today's preservation methods, a donated

The doctors at transplant centers assess patients before adding them to the waiting list.

heart, once removed, must be transplanted within four hours; a lung, within six hours; and a pancreas, within twelve. A kidney, bathed in preservatives, can sit around on ice for a maximum of forty-eight hours. Livers have longer lives. Once a liver has been cooled and drained of blood, it can stay in a plastic bag on ice until it is needed.

Recovery

Recovery rate is affected by what type of organ you had transplanted and by your medical condition. In general, a heart recipient will take longer to recover than a kidney recipient. Although a few lucky recipients recover quickly, problems—organ rejection and infection—are frequent.

Rejection

Your body is extremely choosy about what it lets inside. Your immune system, which protects your body from foreign matter, will attack and destroy anything it doesn't recognize as belonging to you. In doing so, it fights disease-causing viruses and bacteria.

This means that your immune system sees a transplanted organ as an unwanted visitor. Not knowing the organ is good for you, the immune system will start attacking the new organ within a few days of the transplant. This is called organ rejection.

In order to combat rejection, recipients must take anti-rejection drugs, also called immunosuppressants. Even with these drugs, there is still a chance of rejection. Usually, changing drugs or dosages can solve the problem. But in some extreme cases there is total rejection. In such a case, you might need to have a retransplant using another donor organ.

Infection

While antirejection drugs stop your immune system from attacking your new organ, they also stop it from its real job: fighting viruses and infections. This can put you—and sometimes your new organ—at risk of acquiring an infection.

Another downside to immunosuppressants is their side effects. Depending on the drugs and the dosage—the average heart recipient, for example, must take thirty pills a day for the rest of his or her life—such side effects can include nightmares, memory loss, excessive hair growth, weight increase, and even cancer.

Whose Heart Is This Anyway?

Studies show that, at first, many transplant recipients refer to their new organs as "the heart" or "the lung" instead of "my heart" or "my lung." Many also can't help wondering if their new organ has some characteristics of the person who donated it. This phenomenon is especially common with people who get heart transplants. This is because in most cultures, the heart is symbolically linked to a person's passions. In order to discourage such fantasizing, transplant programs keep most information about a

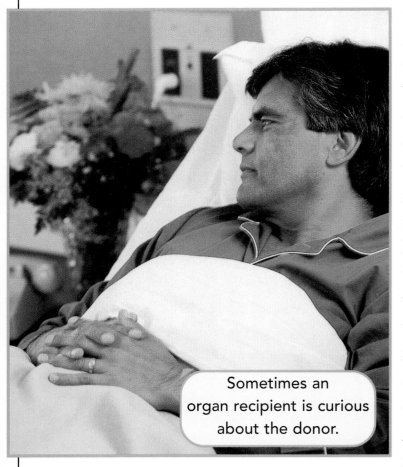

Sometimes an organ recipient is curious about the donor.

donor secret. Sometimes an organ recipient will want to find out about the donor or meet the donor's family. This is rarely allowed. Usually, however, the transplant center will deliver an unsigned letter from the recipient to the donor's family. Although it might stir up painful memories, many families find it comforting to know that the death of their loved one brought life to someone else.

CHAPTER 2

HISTORY OF TRANSPLANTING

The first mention of a transplant dates back to the second century BC. Asked to prove what a medical genius he was, a Chinese physician named Pien Ch'iao exchanged the hearts of two of his patients. In Europe, 700 years later, two physicians named Cosmos and Damian came across a man whose leg had just been amputated. To ease his suffering, they transplanted the leg of a dead soldier. This and other miraculous deeds led Cosmos and Damian to be declared Christian saints.

The scientific progress made over the following centuries transformed myth into medical reality. Experiments with animal organs were taking place at the end of the nineteenth century. The early twentieth century saw the birth of artificial organs. By the middle of the twentieth century, new surgical techniques and breakthrough medicines had made transplant surgery a reality.

People with damaged kidneys undergo dialysis for the rest of their lives unless they get a transplant.

Artificial Organs

Before doctors began using human organs for transplantation, they often used artificial organs—man-made devices that replaced the body's normal functions when organs were lost because of injury or illness. Although some served as permanent replacements, most were temporary substitutes until a living organ became available.

The earliest artificial organs were artificial kidneys. These devices got rid of waste that clogged up the blood of people with damaged kidneys. First, the patient's blood is pumped through the artificial kidney and filtered through a process called dialysis or hemodialysis. Until recently, if you needed dialysis, you had to go to the hospital three times a week and be hooked up to a kidney machine for four to six hours. You would have to do this for the rest of your life, or until you could have a kidney transplant.

In the 1980s, a new procedure became available called continuous ambulatory peritoneal dialysis (CAPD). Patients who choose CAPD don't have to be hooked up to machines and can undergo dialysis in their own homes. Although it means being hooked up to tubes several times a day, home dialysis can be done while you're sleeping. It also takes less time, allows you greater movement, and is half the cost of traditional dialysis.

DR. THOMAS STARZL

Thomas Starzl was to become a priest when, at the age of twenty, his mother died of breast cancer. Vowing to stop death in its tracks, Thomas decided to become a doctor instead. At twenty-six, he entered the almost unknown field of transplantation. In 1963, Starzl performed the world's first liver transplant. This surgery was so technically tricky that for years—until Starzl himself invented a procedure that made the operation less risky—only two other doctors in the world would try it. For many years, Starzl would operate for three days straight because nobody else could do what he could. He developed intricate transplant techniques and immunosuppressive drugs.

Now in his early seventies, the man many call the "finest surgeon of the twentieth century" is no longer operating. (Funnily enough, Starzl claims to have hated surgery with a passion.) Yet he is still very active in transplant research. His latest theory implies that planting "tolerant" cells into the body's immune system would prevent it from fighting the alien organ. If such a theory becomes reality, it could mean good news for transplant patients: no more immunosuppressive drugs.

Another early innovation was the iron lung. Invented in 1928 by Philip Drinker and Louis A. Shaw, it was the first commonly used machine capable of artificial respiration. It was used by patients who had trouble breathing on their own. The iron lung was a large metal tank. If your lungs weren't working well, you would lie in the tank, with only your head sticking out. A rubber collar would go around your neck so that no air could leak out. Air pumped in and out of the tank forced your chest to rise and fall, making you breathe in and out.

A similar invention was the heart-lung machine, developed in 1953, by Dr. John Gibbon of Philadelphia. When your heart stops beating and your lungs stop working, the heart-lung machine tem-

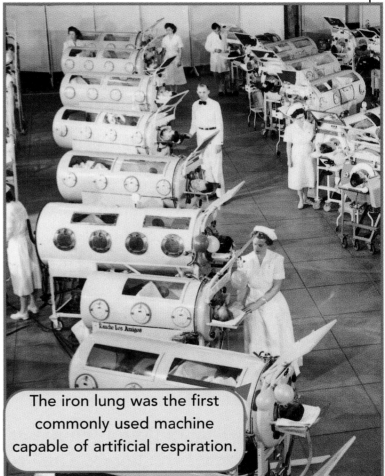

The iron lung was the first commonly used machine capable of artificial respiration.

porarily takes over. This invention was a big breakthrough for open-heart surgery, allowing surgeons more time to operate. Before the heart-lung machine, doctors had to perform heart surgery in under ten minutes. If your heart stopped for longer, you would be permanently brain damaged.

A more permanent solution is the artificial heart, developed in 1957 by Willem Kolff, a Dutch-born doctor. The artificial heart was tested in animals before it was first used on a human patient in 1969. Made out of polyurethane, plastic, and titanium, artificial hearts work just like natural hearts, pumping blood to the lungs and body. They are used in severely ill patients waiting for heart transplants. Barney Clark, the first recipient of a permanently transplanted artificial heart in 1982, died 112 days after the operation; his immune system rejected the organ. After Clark, other patients received artificial heart transplants. However, the longest any of these patients survived was 620 days.

In the 1990s, scientists tried making artificial hearts powered by an electric motor inside the body. Doctors hoped that, in the future, this improved machine could become a permanent replacement for a diseased natural heart.

A Family Affair

Historically, an organ donor tended to be a member of the recipient's immediate family. This was for two reasons. First, family members have similar genes, meaning that their organs and immune systems have many common elements. A recipient's body is much more likely to accept a genetically similar organ than a completely alien organ donated by a stranger. When transplanting a kidney from a brother to a sister or a single lung from a father to a daughter, the chances of a successful transplant are much higher. With both identical and fraternal twins, success rates are especially high. The second reason for family donations is that before donor campaigns and programs came into being, there was no supply of living human organs. In most cases, only a family member would agree to risk his or her life by donating an organ.

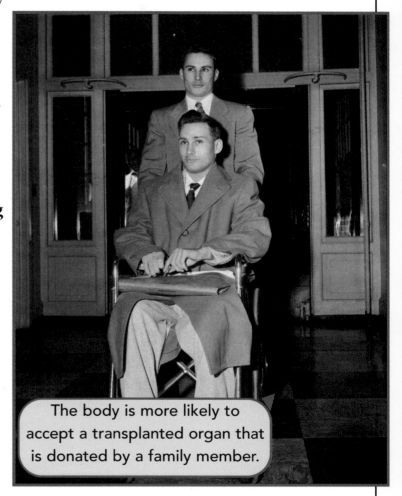

The body is more likely to accept a transplanted organ that is donated by a family member.

The First Transplant

In 1954, kidney disease forced Richard Herrick to quit his job, although he was only twenty-four years old. There seemed to be no treatment for his condition. Dr. Joseph Murray saw Richard's situation as a rare opportunity to avoid organ rejection. This is because the patient had an identical twin brother, Ronald, who offered to donate one of his two kidneys to Richard. Since they had the same biological makeup, Richard's immune system would react to his brother's kidney as if it were his own. This is why when Dr. Murray transplanted Ronald's kidney into Richard, no rejection occurred. Not only did this successful transplant provide Richard with eight additional healthy years of life, but it was a first in the history of medicine, proving that transplantation was a potential treatment for life-threatening organ diseases.

A Common Occurrence

After Dr. Murray's breakthrough, the new task at hand was how to stop bodies from rejecting new organs. As we saw earlier in the book, this problem was overcome with the discovery of antirejection drugs.

Kidneys were the first organs to be transplanted. They are still the organs most frequently transplanted, although heart, liver, pancreas, and even lung transplants have become increasingly commonplace. With scientists constantly doing new research, innovations in transplantation occur all the time. Recent advances in transplant surgery include the transplant of several organs at the same time, transplantation of a piece of an adult organ into a child, and—as we will see in the following chapter—the controversial idea of transplanting animal organs into humans.

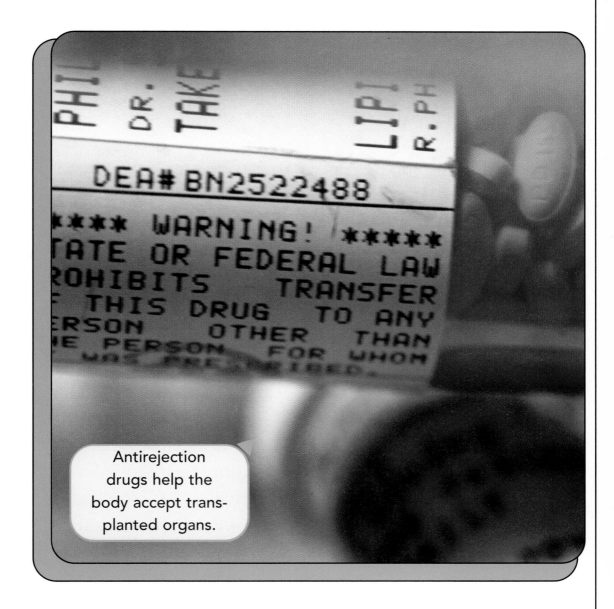

Antirejection drugs help the body accept transplanted organs.

CHAPTER 3

LOOKING INTO THE FUTURE

Because the difference between the number of organs donated and the number of people waiting for organs is so vast and continues to grow, transplant scientists have been looking for alternative ways of saving people's lives in the future. Some of these methods are considered controversial. See what you think.

Animal Organs

Since the beginning of the century, transplant scientists have been toying with the possibility of xenotransplantation—the process of transplanting animal organs into human beings. For a long time, scientists believed that monkey organs could be used because monkeys and humans are incredibly similar. However, transplanting monkey organs into humans has always failed. Many scientists believe that this is because a transplanted animal organ leads to hyperacute rejection, in which proteins in the human body rapidly attack and kill foreign cells. This is why when you put a normal pig heart into a human body, within fifteen minutes it will turn black and stop working. In order to trick these protein cells, scientists have tried injecting human genes into animals, creating animals that are transgenic. In doing so, they hope to create animal organs similar to those of humans, i.e., organs that won't be rejected.

ETHICAL DILEMMA

Is it right to use animals for experimental purposes? Is it cruel to breed abnormal pigs and throw away the ones that "don't work"?

REASONS FOR

Companies and laboratories that use animals for scientific experiments are permitted to do so, provided that the animals are kept in healthy conditions and are not caused to suffer.

The scientific community argues that there is a difference between rational humans and nonrational animals. Humans are thus a "higher" species whose lives are more important. In order for science to advance, for human lives to be improved and saved, experiments must be carried out on animals. It is better to sacrifice animal lives than to sacrifice human lives.

REASONS AGAINST

Animal rights activists claim that many animals are kept in artificial conditions such as tiny pens where they are isolated, drugged, and confined. They argue that many of these experiments are cruel.

Animal rights activists argue that all living creatures deserve equal respect and treatment. All life is sacred.

These days the greatest hopes—in terms of transgenic animals—lie with pigs. They are plentiful and they breed easily. Not only have pigs and people lived side by side for centuries, but pigs are also biologically similar to us. As such, pig-to-human transplants may soon be saving thousands of lives a year. Already, two biotechnology companies, Nextran and Imutran, are in a race to make the perfect pig. Over the last four years, they have met with some success. Today they have created transgenic pigs whose organs—transplanted into baboons—have functioned normally for up to ninety-nine days. At the same time, their success has raised many medical and ethical issues.

Saved by a Pig

In the fall of 1997, nineteen-year-old Robert Pennington was working at a carpet store in Garland, Texas, when he came down with what he thought was the flu. Three weeks later, still feeling sick, he noticed that the whites of his eyes had turned yellow. Tests carried out by transplant surgeon Dr. Marlon Levy revealed that Robert had fulminate hepatic failure, or sudden death of the liver. If Robert didn't receive a transplant, in a few days he would be dead.

TRANSGENIC PIGS

Nextran is a biotechnology company that breeds "perfect pigs"—animals with human genes whose organs can be transplanted into people. Making such a creature begins with a technician giving a 300-pound pregnant sow a tranquilizer. When she dozes off, he cuts her open to remove her newly fertilized eggs. These are placed under a high-powered microscope where, with a needle finer than a strand of hair, a single human gene is injected into each egg. Afterward, each egg will be implanted into a foster mother sow. Around 115 days later, the foster mother pig will give birth to a litter of piglets. After being tagged, the ends of their tails will be snipped off and sent to a laboratory for testing. Scientists hope that one will contain the precious gene that will fool the human immune system into accepting pig organs.

For every 100 gene-altered eggs, twenty piglets will be born. Of those twenty, only one will be transgenic. The other nineteen will be killed.

The greatest hope for xenotransplantation lies with pigs.

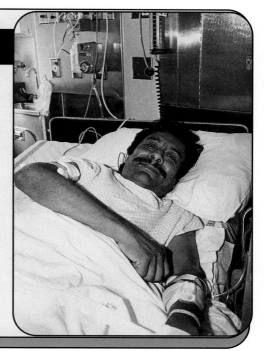

Is it right to start mixing species? Injecting human genes into pigs? Transplanting pig organs into human beings? In doing so, are doctors "playing God"?

Doctors need young, healthy organs for transplants. Even if every person who died donated his or her organs, there still wouldn't be enough to meet the demand. Is xenotransplantation the answer?

The liver's job is to clean poisonous substances from the blood. When it stops working, poisons build up in the bloodstream and travel to the brain, which swells until the patient falls into a coma and dies. Within twenty-four hours of his arrival at Baylor University Medical Center in Dallas, Robert was showing symptoms of severe poisoning.

Because of his critical condition, Robert was placed at the top of the clinic's transplant list. Unfortunately, no livers were available. Prompted by the urgency of the situation, Dr. Levy proposed a highly experimental procedure: Robert would be hooked up to a Nextran pig liver through which his blood would be circulated. Hopefully the pig liver outside the body would keep Robert alive until a human liver could be found for transplantation.

Robert was the first candidate for government-approved testing of this new procedure. When he could no longer eat and breathe on his own, a four-month-old 118-pound transgenic pig named Sweetie Pie was readied for surgery in Baylor's animal laboratory. Dr. Levy removed Sweetie Pie's two-pound liver, covered it with a towel, and put it next to Robert's bed. Tubes ran from the liver in and out of Robert, pumping poisoned blood out and clean blood back in. The pig's liver was still working just fine six and a half hours later, when a human liver was found 250 miles away, in Houston.

The Money Motivation

There is one big difference between human organs and pig organs. For the most part—at least in North America and Europe—human organs are donated. Pig organs, however, are sold. Doctors and scientists want to save people's lives. But the race to make the perfect pig is also

motivated by the fact that its makers—and everybody else involved in transplantation—stand to make a lot of money.

If successful, the market for transgenic organs could be worth $6 billion in a few years. Producers of transgenic pigs could make millions. So would the big pharmaceutical companies who make antirejection drugs. And so would hospitals and surgeons. With the average cost of a transplant now over $250,000, if every American who needed a transplant could suddenly get one—courtesy of the perfect pig—patients would be paying $20.3 billion a year instead of the $2.9 billion they spend today.

It is the potential profit involved that makes some people nervous. Concerned groups—such as the Campaign for Responsible Transplantation, a group of scientists and public-health professionals—have asked that the government ban xenotransplant research. They worry that with so much money to be made and so much demand for organs, transgenic pig organs might be catapulted onto the transplant market before all the potential and possibly catastrophic health and safety issues have been sufficiently explored.

Five Arguments Against Xenotransplantation

1. Since 1906, there have been more than fifty-five animal-to-human organ transplants. All

were unsuccessful, resulting in the suffering and death of the patients and donor animals.

2. Xenotransplantation could prove even more expensive than human-to-human transplantation. Aside from the $250,000 transplant fee, there are the costs of breeding, housing, feeding, medicating, transporting, and disposing of the remains of transgenic animals.

3. Xenotransplantation could pose a major health risk. Animals have specific viruses that can spread to humans through transplantation. When you transplant living animal organs into humans, you bypass natural barriers (such as skin) that prevent infection, allowing diseases to spread from animals to humans. Just look at what happened when a virus that was originally found only in monkeys came into contact with the human race: the AIDS epidemic.

4. Viruses that are harmless to animals can be deadly when transmitted to humans. The human flu virus of 1918 that killed more than 20 million people worldwide was related to a swine flu virus. Unfortunately, to date, there is no way to detect unknown pig viruses.

5. Certain major differences between pigs and people—such as differences in life span, blood

ETHICAL DILEMMA

A LIFE SAVED = A POSSIBLE EPIDEMIC

Is it better to save a human life and risk possible contamination of an entire society at a future point in time?

To justify any experiment on humans, scientists must show that the benefits to the patient outweigh the risks. But with xenotransplants, this rule of medical ethics goes out the window. In letting a human receive a transplanted heart from a pig, the patient benefits, while society risks the possible spread of viruses. An individual patient can sign a consent form in which he or she agrees to take a medical risk because without the xenotransplant he or she is going to die anyway. In the case of animal-to-human transplants, it's as if the patient is signing a consent form accepting the risk for the entire human race.

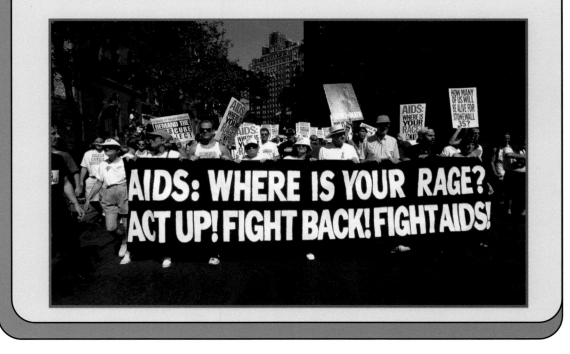

pressure, heart rate, hormones, and immune systems—make rejection of even transgenic pig organs a serious problem. In order for a pig organ not to be rejected, massive doses of immunosuppressive drugs would be necessary, the side effects of which could be dangerous, or even fatal.

6. Government regulatory bodies such as the Food and Drug Administration (FDA) promise to monitor and set up safety rules concerning xenotransplantation. However, in the past, the United States government was not able to successfully protect innocent people from being infected with AIDS-contaminated blood transfusions or from exposure to dangerous chemicals during the Persian Gulf War.

CHAPTER 4

ORGAN DONORS

Because people are living longer, never before has there been such a need for new organs. Although over 20,000 transplants are performed in the United States every year, 5,000 people die every year waiting for a transplant. The shortage of donors is so severe that doctors are forced to take greater risks. Aside from transplanting organs from older patients (in 1988, only 2 percent of heart donors were over fifty years old; today that number is 10 percent), doctors are using organs taken from cocaine users. They have also been known to transplant hearts and lungs that, having been outside of the donor's body for more than four to six hours, have begun to deteriorate. The result can be that an organ saves a life but will cause trouble later.

The problem is that the number of donors—mostly people who die suddenly—is less than 10,000 people a year. And although it sounds strange to say this, better

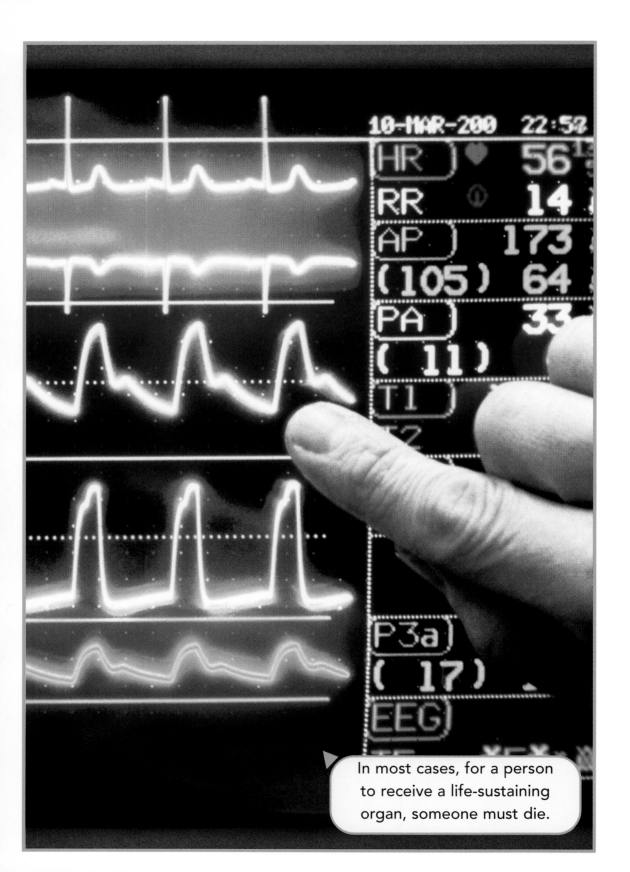

In most cases, for a person to receive a life-sustaining organ, someone must die.

health care and new surgery techniques are saving more people who, in the past, may have been suitable donors. Even worse for those awaiting transplants is the fact that stricter seat belt laws, successful anti-drinking-and-driving campaigns, and air bags in cars have meant that fewer people die in car crashes. This, too, means fewer donors.

When Your Life Is Saved by Death

To date, kidneys are the only organs that can be donated by a living donor. In most cases, for a person to receive an organ that will sustain their life, someone else must die. And it is preferable that this other person die in the prime of life, not from old age or from some terrible disease.

It is not uncommon for some patients who desperately need an organ to fantasize about accidents that will lead to their receiving an organ that will be "theirs." Such thoughts lead to guilty feelings, although obviously, they in no way influence what will happen to another person. Furthermore, studies show that most people like the idea that after their death their organs will give life to another person.

The Definition of Death

Did you ever ask yourself what it means to be dead? The actual state of being "dead" can mean many things to many people, depending on your culture, religion, or personal

Your decision to become an organ donor is noted on your driver's license.

beliefs. Before, if your heart, lungs, liver, and other vital organs stopped working, they stopped for good, and so did you. Today, however, machines can keep your organs "working" for a very long time. Hence, when doctors talk about being "dead," they often mean being "brain dead." When your brain dies, so do your thoughts and your body functions. However, your heart may still continue to pump. Some people—particularly inhabitants of Asian countries such as Japan and Indonesia—have problems with this notion. They feel that you are not dead until every sign of life has been extinguished.

Deciding to Donate

When questioned, most Americans are overwhelmingly in favor of donating their organs. The problem is often getting people to make the decision to donate and then sharing that decision with their families and their doctors.

Much of the difficulty is due to lack of awareness. Neither the United States government nor the medical community has done all it can to encourage people to become organ donors. Currently, only 20 percent of people who die "healthy" have made arrangements to donate their organs. This is too bad when you consider that 85 percent of the population supports organ donation. In some countries,

ETHICAL DILEMMA

Is asking a grieving family for their dying member's organs a good or insensitive thing to do?

Obviously, the best solution is to educate people so that they have chosen to become donors before these kinds of situations occur. However, health care staff are often unwilling or unable to approach families to discuss organ donation and obtain consent. What helps is when hospitals have rules about staff being trained to deal with such delicate situations. In the Canadian province of Ontario, for example, by law all hospitals must have procedures whereby staff identify potential donors and make their families aware of organ donation.

governments have stepped in and created laws that automatically make all citizens donors, unless they specify otherwise—on their driver's license for instance. In Austria, for example, there were suddenly four times as many organs available once an "automatic consent" law was passed. If a similar law were passed in the United States, 75 percent of the adult population would become potential organ donors.

As things now stand, doctors and hospitals have a complicated role to play. Obviously, in some cases—such as hospital staff approaching the grief-stricken parents of a teenager who has just been killed in a car crash and asking for an organ donation—the whole organ donor issue can be very complex. There have been examples of hospital staff bungling the job by approaching a potential donor's family in the wrong way, at the wrong time.

Should Organ Donors Be Given Rewards?

Some people think that more people would donate organs if they were given a specific incentive to do so: money. Both state governments and health organizations have considered plans for "rewarding" families of organ donors. The state of Pennsylvania is considering paying families of organ donors $300 to help cover the donors' funeral costs. Although the money will be paid directly to the funeral homes, some people worry about the principle of exchanging money for organs. They fear this will open up an organ market—where organs are bought and sold. Because so many people desperately need organs, they would pay any price for them.

Until now, such a market—and any program that offers money for human body parts—has always been seen as ethically wrong. In fact, United States law prohibits the buying and selling of organs.

Many people who are willing to donate their organs fail to share their wishes with family members.

MATCHING DONORS AND RECIPIENTS

In 1998, in order to make sure no opportunities for donation were being missed, the United States Department of Health and Human Resources (HHS) issued a regulation requiring hospitals to notify organ procurement organizations (OPOs) of all deaths and imminent deaths. To make things easier, all such information will be placed on an Internet database system created by the United Network for Organ Sharing (UNOS).

This system, called UNetsm, is used by both transplant hospitals and OPOs in charge of recovering organs. Logging onto a Web site, hospitals put patients on the UNOS transplant waiting list. When an organ becomes available, the organization that recovers it logs onto the same site to match the organ to the proper patient. The hospital is then contacted and the patient gets the organ he or she needs.

The International Organ Market: True Stories

The Philippines

Romeo Roga earned $1.25 a day lifting sacks of rice at Manila's harbor. When his infant son came down with the measles, there was no way Romeo could pay the hospital bills. Desperate, Romeo called his stepfather, who told him he could easily make $2,000. All he had to do was sell his kidney. Not wanting his son to die, Romeo sold his kidney. His son died anyway. And with a family of five to feed, the money lasted only two years. Romeo went

---

ETHICAL DILEMMA

If paying for organs did create an organ market, and if this market did away with the shortage of organs, would it be worth it?

The experience in developing countries might make those who favor an organ market think twice. In such countries, people who are desperate for money sell their kidneys without knowing the risks involved. Rich people can buy all the organs they need or want; those less fortunate can't get any at all.

---

back to his same job, but with one kidney, he finds the heavy work exhausting and is not sure if he can keep doing it.

Romeo's story—and too many others like it—created much controversy in the Philippines. The Roman Catholic Church said that the organ trade was unethical, exploiting the poor and uneducated. Eventually, the government banned any living organ

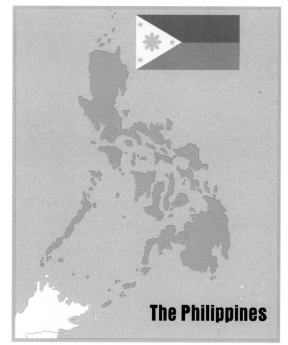

The Philippines

Buying and selling organs: Is it right or wrong? Are parts of our body really just spare parts that can be bought and sold? Or are they somehow different and special?

IT'S RIGHT

Human labor is sold, sex is sold, sperm and eggs are sold, even babies are sold through international adoption. So why not kidneys?

An organ is just an organ, a heart is just a pump, a kidney is just a filter. Isn't it better to use them than to waste them when lives are at stake?

IT'S WRONG

Religious, cultural, and spiritual beliefs are sacrificed due to greed, dire necessity, and extreme market demand (desperately sick buyers and desperately poor sellers).

An organ is a living, spiritualized part of a person that some people want to take with them when they die.

donations by nonrelatives. However, many doctors, as well as people waiting for kidneys, were against the ban. After all, with patients willing to pay any price for kidneys and donors desperate to escape poverty, it's a win-win situation. Isn't it?

Japan

In Japan, most people don't believe the theory that when your brain dies, the rest of you is dead, too. This means that there

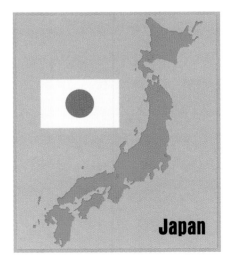

Japan

are very few donors in Japan. For many years, rich Japanese people in search of transplants hired criminal gangs known as the "body mafia" to find kidney donors in other countries. Desperate patients have been known to pay up to $30,000 for a kidney.

China

China is the only country where transplant organs are still taken from executed prisoners. Most of these organs are sold for huge sums to "medical visitors" from Hong Kong, Taiwan, and Singapore.

Recently, China began a tough anticrime campaign. As a result, many more people are jailed and executed. Some people have even been executed for petty theft and for cheating on their taxes. It is estimated that the Chinese government takes organs from 2,000 executed prisoners a year. None of these prisoners ever signs a consent form. Some experts believe that China is doing this so that it will have more organs to sell.

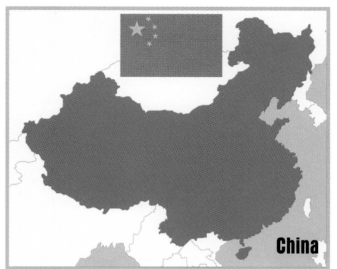

China

India

In India, most donors are poor people who sell one of their kidneys. Most buyers are rich people from neighboring Arab countries. In 1997, the Indian government made selling and buying organs illegal. However, this only made the trade go underground, where it is controlled by criminal gangs. The criminal aspect of the organ trade is a serious problem. It is not uncommon to hear stories of

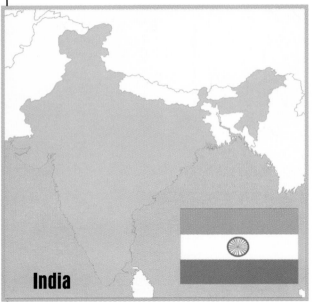

India

organ theft. And as unbelievable as these stories may seem, many are true. One young woman, who went to a clinic with stomach pains, was told she needed to have a bladder stone removed. When she woke up after the operation, one of her kidneys was "missing."

Brazil

In Brazil, it is also common to buy and sell kidneys. Only there, people try to make it look like a "gift" between two supposed "relatives." Even though doctors might suspect this isn't the case, they rarely ask questions.

Brazil

Instead of following India's example and banning the buying and selling of organs, the Brazilian government created a law that automatically made all Brazilians donors when they die. It was hoped that the law would make so many organs available for transplant that there would be no need for anybody to purchase them. However, many Brazilians worried that greedy medical staff would take advantage of the new law. They imagined ambulance workers being paid to lie and say a patient had died, just so somebody could have their organ. Because of such worries, the law was never passed.

CHAPTER 5

ORGAN RECIPIENTS

The severe shortage of organs and the growing number of people who need them create a whole series of issues that revolve around who receives organs, where, when, and how. Currently, 50,000 Americans need a new heart. Around 95 percent of them will die without getting one. In 1998, of the lucky 7,683 patients whose condition was serious enough to get them on the national transplant waiting list, only 2,340 received new hearts.

Making It onto the Waiting List

The national organ recipient waiting list is organized by the United Network for Organ Sharing (UNOS). Factors that determine who makes it onto the list—and what their place in line is—include the seriousness of a patient's illness and their blood type. During the wait, one patient's condition might worsen, causing him or her to be bumped

A transplant team is responsible for conserving scarce organs for the patients who will benefit the most from the operation.

up closer to the top of the list. Meanwhile, if another patient's condition improves, he or she will become a less urgent case and move down the list.

Once on a list, things don't get easier. A transplant team will agonize over any decision that might cause them to delay or even refuse necessary surgery for a patient. Their goal is to help people get transplants, not turn them down. At the same time, they have a responsibility to conserve scarce organs for those who will benefit from them most.

If it is discovered that you have a problem with drugs or alcohol, you might be turned down for a transplant. Or your transplant will be delayed until you have had treatment for your addiction. Many surgeons think it is a waste to operate when a drug or alcohol problem could threaten the success of the operation and subsequent recovery.

Who's First?
Where You Live versus How Sick You Are

Up until recently, if an organ donor died in a hospital in Santa Fe, New Mexico, would-be recipients living in Santa Fe would be the first ones in line for a new organ. Next in line were those living in areas surrounding Santa Fe, followed by those living in the state of New Mexico, and then those from neighboring states. The closer you lived to a transplant centers, the better your chance of receiving a transplant.

In the days when transplant surgery was rare and only a handful of hospitals were equipped to perform such operations, this procedure worked well. But as waiting lists grew longer and more transplant centers were created, a situation of inequality emerged. Regions with smaller populations or a larger concentration of transplant centers had more organs available than those with large populations or fewer transplant centers. A recent HHS study found that waiting times for new organs ranged from forty-six days in Iowa to 721 days in western Pennsylvania.

Because of recent advances, it is not essential for the patient and the organ to be in the same place.

To improve the situation, the HHS created a new set of regulations that came into effect at the end of 1999. With these new regulations, closeness to an organ donor will no longer be a factor. Instead, it will depend on how sick the patient is. This should ensure that people who need transplants the most get them first, no matter where they live. The HHS argued that because new technology keeps organs and patients alive for longer periods, it was no longer essential for both the patient and the organ to be in the same place.

Some members of the medical community are worried about these new regulations. They fear the following problems might emerge:

- Hospitals will unfairly list their patients as sicker than they are so that they will get organs more quickly.

- Organs will needlessly—and expensively—be flown all over the country.

- Large hospitals in big cities with many of the sickest patients would get first choice of available organs. Because of the high cost of transplant operations, these hospitals would make a lot of money, enabling them to update their technology and improve their transplant facilities. At the same time, smaller transplant centers in towns or rural areas would lose money and patients, forcing them to close.

- Organs would be wasted by transplants

into patients who are so sick that their chances of recovery are extremely small. Meanwhile, healthier patients with better chances of survival would be forced to wait longer and risk getting sicker or dying.

Stiff Competition

At times, the severe organ shortage raises the issue of who gets one, who doesn't, and when (if ever) into a competition. Because of this, transplant teams have to decide if a patient will make a good recipient. This means making sure they don't have an illness that is so severe that it will affect the success of the transplant. Because organs are so valuable, they must be used so that the greatest possible benefit results. Few doctors

WALTER PAYTON

In 1998, Walter Payton, the Chicago Bears' Hall of Fame running back and the NFL's career rushing leader was diagnosed with a rare liver disease. Payton was forty-five. The only chance he had of living was to receive a liver transplant. Unfortunately, while waiting, Payton developed a severe cancer that was a complication of his disease. The cancer spread so rapidly that doctors had to rule out a transplant. On November 1, 1999, Walter Payton died.

"The best gift I ever got was on June 8, 1995, when an organ donor gave me and five other patients at Baylor University Medical Center in Dallas the organs we needed to live. I guess you could say I got another time at bat."

Baseball great—and liver recipient—Mickey Mantle

would suggest a transplant if it was likely to be a failure because there are always others waiting who might benefit more.

Transplant teams weigh a lot of factors when deciding who gets a transplant and when. Although, in general, teams try to transplant those whose lives are most in danger, there are other important factors as well. There must be an acceptable match in blood type between the donor and recipient. For lung transplants, the donor's lung must fit the size of the recipient's chest.

For patients who are so ill that they must be hospitalized while waiting for a possible organ, there can be a feeling of competitiveness. Who will get an organ first? Although teams try to avoid such situations—by minimizing the number of

SHOULD MURDERERS HAVE TRANSPLANTS, TOO?

In 1968, James Earl Ray shot and killed civil rights leader Martin Luther King Jr. Ray is in a Tennessee jail, where he is serving a ninety-nine-year prison term. He also has hepatitis, which doctors say will kill him in a matter of months unless he gets a new liver. The question is, does he deserve it?

YES

A Pennsylvania hospital will put Ray on its waiting list provided that someone comes up with $250,000—the deposit necessary for transplant patients without medical insurance.

It is the hospital's view that criminals should be treated in the same way as any other patient.

SHOULD MURDERERS HAVE TRANSPLANTS, TOO?

NO

The reality is that for every sick person whose life is saved by a transplant, another dies for lack of an available organ.

Protesters argue that it is better to save the life of a person who is likely to make a positive contribution to society.

Saying good-bye to a loved one is difficult—
no matter what he or she did during life.

people on a waiting list who are competing for the same type of donor organ—this is sometimes unavoidable. One hospital might end up with several would-be lung recipients who have the same-sized lungs and identical blood types. In this situation, the person who is the most ill is generally considered first. This can be hard for the other person, who might have been waiting longer. Especially since the next time a suitable organ comes along, their health might have taken a turn for the worse.

Do some people have more right to a transplant than others? What do you think?

GLOSSARY

"brain dead" When the brain completely stops working and can't be revived.

consent Permission.

cyclosporine The most commonly used antirejection drug.

dialysis Procedure whereby blood leaves the body, is cleansed, and returns to the body.

donor Someone who gives (an organ) without being paid.

epidemic Massive outbreak of a disease.

gene Section of a chromosome. Each is responsible for an inherited characteristic.

heart Organ responsible for pumping blood to the rest of the body.

hepatitis A serious liver disease.

hyperacute rejection Severe and immediate rejection of an organ.

ORGAN TRANSPLANT

immunosuppressant   Substance, or drug, that prevents the immune system from attacking foreign material.

kidneys   Organs responsible for filtering waste out of the body.

liver   Organ responsible for cleansing blood.

lung   Organ responsible for respiration (breathing).

pancreas   Organ responsible for digestion.

recipient   Person who receives (an organ).

transgenic   Occurs when genes from more than one source are incorporated, or mixed, together.

xenotransplantation   The process of transplanting organs from one species into another.

FOR MORE
INFORMATION

In the United States

American Kidney Fund
6110 Executive Boulevard, Suite 1010
Rockville, MD 20852
(800) 638-8299 or (301) 881-3052
Web site: http://www.akfinc.org/

Children's Organ Transplant Association (COTA)
2501 COTA Drive
Bloomington, IN 47403
(800) 366-COTA

Department of Health and Human Services (HHS)
Division of Transplantation

ORGAN TRANSPLANT

5600 Fishers Lane, Room 4-81
Rockville, MD 20857
(301) 443-7577
Web site: http://www.organdonor.gov

LifeGift Organ Donation Center
5615 Kirby Drive, Suite 900
Houston, TX 77005
(713) 523-4438
Web site: http://www.lifegift.org/

The Mickey Mantle Foundation
8080 N. Central Expressway, Suite 800
Dallas, TX 75206-1887
(800) 477-MICK (6425) or (214) 987-7977

National Foundation for Transplants
1102 Brookfield, Suite 200
Memphis, TN 38119
(800) 489-3863 or (901) 684-1697
Web site: http://www.transplants.org

UNOS/National Transplant Research Center
100 Boulders Parkway, Suite 500
Richmond, VA 23225
(804) 330-8546

FOR MORE INFORMATION

In Canada

Canadian Institute for Health Information (CIHI)
377 Dalhousie Street, Suite 200
Ottawa, ON K1N 9N8
(613) 241-7860, ext. 4069
Web site: http://www.cihi.ca/

London Health Sciences Center
800 Commissioners Road East
London, ON N6A 4G5
(519) 685-8500
Web site: http://www.lhsc.on.ca/

Web Sites

TransWeb
http://www.transweb.org
Educational site about organ donation and transplantation housed at the University of Michigan Medical Center.

United Network for Organ Sharing (UNOS)
Web site: http://www.unos.org
Site of the national network in charge of organ donation and transplantation policy and information.

FOR FURTHER READING

Caplan, Arthur L., and Daniel H. Coelho (eds). *The Ethics of Organ Transplants: The Current Debate.* Amherst, NY: Prometheus Books, 1999.

Facklam, Margery. *Spare Parts for People.* New York: Harcourt Brace, 1996.

Ribal, Lizzy. *Lizzy Gets a New Liver.* Louisville, KY: Bridge Resources, 1997.

Spielman, Bethany (ed.). *Organ and Tissue Donation: Ethical, Legal, and Policy Issues.* Carbondale, IL: Southern Illinois University Press, 1996.

Walton, Karen. *How Will They Get That Heart Down Your Throat? A Child's View of Transplants.* Berkeley, CA: E.M. Press, 1999.

Youngner, Stuart J., et al. (eds.) *Organ Transplantation: Meanings and Realities.* Madison, WI: University of Wisconsin Press, 1996.

INDEX

CREDITS

About the Author

Adam Winters lives in Texas, where he raises cattle and grows chili peppers. He is also a part-time journalist.

Photo Credits

Cover by © Bettmann/Corbis; p. 2 © Uniphoto; p. 6 © Scott Thode/International Stock; p. 9 © Peter Langone/International Stock; p. 10 © Charles Gupton/Uniphoto; p. 11 © James J. Broderick/International Stock; p.14 © Adam Smith Productions/FPG; p. 16 © Paul Almasy/Corbis; pp. 19, 21 © Bettmann/Corbis; p. 23 © Phillip James Corwin/Corbis; p. 28 by John Bacolo; p. 29 © Shelley Gazin/Corbis; p. 30 © T. Stephen Thompson/Uniphoto; p. 33 © Michael S.Yamashi/Corbis; p. 36 © Telegraph Colour Library/FPG; p. 41 © Mark Reinstein/FPG; p. 49 Uniphoto; p. 51 © Noble Stock/International Stock; p. 53 © Archive Photos; p. 54 © Frank Capri/SAGA/Archive Photos; p. 56 © Rick Brady/Uniphoto.

Series Design

Michael Caraleo

Layout

Law Alsobrook

P9-CFT-532

HOME-BAKED GOODNESS

THERE'S MORE TO PUMPKIN
THAN MEETS THE PIE

Steeped in tradition, pumpkin pie has become a symbol of American celebration. Each year, cooks bake over 55 million Libby's Pumpkin Pies, satisfying families with the rich pumpkin taste they know and love. Now you can experience this time-honored ingredient in a variety of baked goods, created for year-round enjoyment. Libby's special tribute to home baking features our Libby's Famous Pumpkin Pies—but that's just the beginning.

This collection offers a windfall of delectable ways to serve Home-Baked Goodness to family and friends—including cakes, breads, cookies and quick-fix treats. All you need is a few basic ingredients and a can of Libby's Pumpkin to create over 60 recipes. With so many delicious choices, you'll turn to these pages again and again for baking inspiration.

 Look for this symbol on certain recipes throughout this book, which means the recipe is at least 25% lower in fat than the original recipe. Each of these recipes lists the amount of calories and fat per serving. Although the recipes marked with this symbol were designed to be lower in fat, any of the desserts and baked goods in this book can be part of a nutritious diet when enjoyed in moderation.

HOME-BAKED GOODNESS

CONTENTS

Pictured on cover: Pumpkin Swirl Breakfast Rolls (see recipe, page 68)

This edition is a revised and enlarged version of the soft-cover Libby's Home-Baked Goodness © Copyright 1995 Nestlé. All rights reserved. Produced by Meredith Custom Publishing, 1912 Grand Ave., Des Moines, Iowa 50309-3379. Canadian BN 12348 2887 RT. Printed in Hong Kong.

LIBBY'S FAMOUS
PUMPKIN PIES
AS EASY AS 1-2-3

Pumpkin pie dates back to Pilgrim times, but it was Libby's that made it famous. In 1950, Libby's Famous Pumpkin Pie recipe first appeared on our canned pumpkin label. Now an American tradition, this best-loved pie comes together in three simple steps: just mix, pour and bake. Also try our Super-Quick recipe, using Libby's Pumpkin Pie Mix, and the Lighter version on pages 6 and 7.

Libby's Famous Pumpkin Pie
(see recipe, page 6)

LIBBY'S FAMOUS PUMPKIN PIE

1 *unbaked* 9-inch (4-cup volume) pie shell
  (see recipe, *page 28*) or two shallow *unbaked*
  9-inch (2-cup volume) pie shells
¾ cup granulated sugar
1 teaspoon ground cinnamon
½ teaspoon salt
½ teaspoon ground ginger
¼ teaspoon ground cloves

2 eggs
1¾ cups (15- or 16-ounce can) LIBBY'S Solid Pack
  Pumpkin
1½ cups (12 fluid-ounce can) CARNATION
  Evaporated Milk
  Whipped cream (optional)
  Chopped nuts (optional)

Combine sugar, cinnamon, salt, ginger and cloves in small bowl. Beat eggs lightly in large bowl. Stir in pumpkin and sugar mixture. Gradually stir in evaporated milk. Pour into pie shell(s). Bake* in preheated 425°F. oven 15 minutes. Reduce temperature to 350°F. Bake 40 to 50 minutes more for one 4-cup volume pie (15 to 20 minutes for 2 shallow pies) or until knife inserted near center comes out clean. Cool on wire rack(s). Garnish with whipped cream and nuts, if desired. Makes 1 or 2 pies (8 servings *each*).   *Pictured on pages 4 and 5.*

LIBBY'S SUPER-QUICK PUMPKIN PIE

1 *unbaked* 9-inch (4-cup volume) pie shell (see
  recipe, *page 28*) or two shallow *unbaked* 9-inch
  (2-cup volume) pie shells

2 eggs
3¼ cups (30-ounce can) LIBBY'S Pumpkin Pie Mix
⅔ cup CARNATION Evaporated Milk

Beat eggs lightly in large bowl. Stir in pumpkin pie mix and evaporated milk. Pour into pie shell(s). Bake* in preheated 425°F. oven 15 minutes. Reduce temperature to 350°F. Bake 50 to 60 minutes more for one 4-cup volume pie (about 30 minutes for 2 shallow pies) or until knife inserted near center comes out clean. Cool on wire rack(s). Makes 1 or 2 pies (8 servings *each*).

*Note: If using a metal or foil pan(s), bake on preheated *heavy* baking sheet.

LIGHTER LIBBY'S FAMOUS PUMPKIN PIE

1 *unbaked* 9-inch (4-cup volume) pie shell
  (see recipe, *page 30*) or two shallow *unbaked*
  9-inch (2-cup volume) pie shells
¾ cup granulated sugar
1 tablespoon cornstarch
1 teaspoon ground cinnamon
½ teaspoon salt

½ teaspoon ground ginger
2 egg whites
1¾ cups (15- or 16-ounce can) LIBBY'S Solid Pack
  Pumpkin
1½ cups (12 fluid-ounce can) CARNATION Evaporated
  Skimmed Milk

Combine sugar, cornstarch, cinnamon, salt and ginger in small bowl. Beat egg whites lightly in large bowl. Stir in pumpkin and sugar mixture. Gradually stir in evaporated skimmed milk. Pour into pie shell(s).

Bake* in preheated 425°F. oven for 15 minutes. Reduce oven temperature to 350°F. Bake for 30 to 40 minutes more for one 4-cup volume pie (15 to 20 minutes for 2 shallow pies) or until knife inserted near center comes out clean. Cool pie(s) on wire rack(s). Makes 1 or 2 pies (8 servings *each*). Per serving (4-cup volume pie): 5 grams fat and 210 calories.

*Note: If using a metal or foil pan(s), bake on preheated *heavy* baking sheet.

PUMPKIN PIE Q & A

With over 55 million LIBBY'S pumpkin pies made each year, it is no surprise that bakers turn to the Libby's Test Kitchen for advice. Here are the answers to the most common pie-making questions:

- How do you tell when a pumpkin pie is done? Insert a knife near the center of the pie (about 1 to 1½ inches from the center). If the knife comes out clean with no custard filling clinging to it, the pie is done.
- Can you freeze a pumpkin pie? No, but you can freeze the filling and pie crust separately (for up to one month). Thaw, stir and pour the filling into the crust, baking as directed. Thaw the crust, too, if prepared in a glass pie plate. Crusts prepared in metal or aluminum pans do not need thawing.
- What causes a pie to crack or pull away from the crust? Overbaking can cause both of these results. Also, make sure your oven rack is centered in the oven (no higher) to avoid a crust from forming on the top of your pie.

SPECIAL-OCCASION DESSERTS

When friends and family gather to celebrate, give them a slice worth remembering. Maple-iced Vermont Spice Cake, Pumpkin Apple Gingerbread and Pumpkin Caramel Flan are just a few of the exquisite desserts in this chapter, each designed to leave a lasting impression. All of the recipes can be made before your guests arrive, so you, too, can relax and join in the festivities.

Vermont Spice Cake
(see recipe, page 10)

VERMONT SPICE CAKE

CAKE

1½ cups granulated sugar
¾ cup (1½ sticks) butter, softened
3 eggs
1½ cups LIBBY'S Solid Pack Pumpkin
1½ teaspoons vanilla extract
½ cup CARNATION Evaporated Milk
¼ cup water
3 cups all-purpose flour
3½ teaspoons baking powder
1½ teaspoons ground cinnamon
1 teaspoon baking soda
¾ teaspoon ground nutmeg
½ teaspoon salt
¼ teaspoon ground cloves
¼ teaspoon ground ginger
Chopped nuts and/or nut halves (optional)

MAPLE FROSTING

1 package (8 ounces) *and* 1 package (3 ounces) cream cheese, softened
⅓ cup butter, softened
3½ cups sifted powdered sugar
2 to 3 teaspoons maple flavoring

FOR CAKE: Beat granulated sugar and butter in large mixer bowl until creamy. Add eggs; beat for 2 minutes. Add pumpkin and vanilla; mix well. Beat in evaporated milk and water.

Combine flour, baking powder, cinnamon, baking soda, nutmeg, salt, cloves and ginger in a large bowl. Beat into pumpkin mixture.

Spread pumpkin mixture evenly into 2 greased and floured 9-inch round cake pans. Bake in preheated 325°F. oven for 35 to 40 minutes or until wooden pick inserted in center comes out clean. Cool in pans on racks for 15 minutes. Remove from pans; cool.

FOR MAPLE FROSTING: Beat cream cheese and butter in large mixer bowl; gradually beat in powdered sugar. Beat in maple flavoring until fluffy.

TO ASSEMBLE: Cut cakes in half horizontally with long serrated knife.* Frost between layers and on top of cake, leaving sides unfrosted. Top with nuts. Store in refrigerator. Makes 12 servings.

*Note: To make a 2-layer cake, frost between layers, over top, and on sides of cake. Garnish with nuts. *Pictured on pages 8 and 9.*

SPECIAL FINISHING TOUCHES

A dusting of powdered sugar or a sprinkling of nuts can turn the most basic dessert into a showpiece. Count on these simple garnishing ideas to dress up your baked goods.

- **Press handfuls of chopped nuts** along the sides of a frosted cake, or just sprinkle them on top. Whole nuts, caramelized nuts and chocolate-dipped nuts also jazz up desserts.

  - **For easy drizzling** with no mess, create a makeshift pastry bag from a heavy-duty zip-top plastic bag. To drizzle chocolate, snip a small hole in a corner of a bag filled with melted NESTLÉ TOLL HOUSE Morsels. Use to write, design or draw, decorating desserts or plates in your own creative way. This makeshift pastry bag works well for icing and jelly designs, too.

  - **Turn to the fruit bowl** for fresh and simple garnishes. Strawberry fans, thinly sliced citrus, assorted berries and kiwi fruit wedges add a burst of color and flavor, too.

- **Edible flowers,** including nasturtiums, pansies and violets, offer simple elegance atop desserts or on dessert plates. Look for edible flowers in supermarkets or local gardens, but be sure they are chemical-free.

  - **Add the look of lace** or a stenciled design atop cakes and cookies with doilies or stencils. Lay the doily or stencil atop the cake or cookie and gently sift powdered sugar or unsweetened cocoa over the top. Carefully remove the doily or stencil to see your work of art. For a striped or checkerboard design, position strips of waxed paper on the cake or cookie and repeat as above.

PUMPKIN APPLE GINGERBREAD

3½ cups all-purpose flour
1 tablespoon baking powder
2½ teaspoons ground ginger
½ teaspoon baking soda
½ teaspoon salt
½ teaspoon pumpkin pie spice
1 cup (2 sticks) butter or margarine, softened
1 cup granulated sugar

½ cup packed brown sugar
4 eggs
1¾ cups (15- or 16-ounce can) LIBBY'S Solid Pack Pumpkin
1 large baking apple (such as pippin or Granny Smith), peeled and shredded (about 1 cup)
½ cup molasses
Powdered sugar
Hard Sauce (recipe follows)

Combine flour, baking powder, ginger, baking soda, salt and pumpkin pie spice in medium bowl.

Beat butter, granulated sugar and brown sugar in large mixer bowl until light and fluffy. Add eggs 2 at a time, beating well after each addition. Beat in pumpkin, apple and molasses. Gradually beat in flour mixture.

Spoon batter into well-greased and floured 12-cup fluted tube pan.* Bake in preheated 350°F. oven for 1 hour or until wooden pick inserted in cake comes out clean. Cool in pan on wire rack for 15 minutes; remove from pan. Dust with powdered sugar. Serve warm with Hard Sauce. Makes 12 servings.

*Note: Recipe also may be made in two 8- or 9-inch round cake pans or one 13 x 9-inch baking pan. Bake in preheated 350°F. oven for 40 to 45 minutes or until wooden pick inserted in cake comes out clean.

FOR HARD SAUCE: Beat 1 cup (2 sticks) softened butter and 2 teaspoons vanilla extract in small mixer bowl until smooth. Gradually beat in 4 cups sifted powdered sugar until fluffy.

Pumpkin Apple Gingerbread

Pumpkin Caramel Flan

¾ cup granulated sugar
4 eggs
1 cup LIBBY'S Solid Pack Pumpkin
⅓ cup honey
1 to 1½ teaspoons pumpkin pie spice

1 teaspoon vanilla extract
½ teaspoon salt
1½ cups (12 fluid-ounce can) CARNATION
    Evaporated Milk
Nasturtium blossoms (optional)

Place 8-inch square baking dish into 13 x 9-inch baking dish; fill outer dish with hot water to ¾-inch depth.

Heat sugar in heavy skillet over medium heat, stirring constantly, until melted and golden brown; pour into square dish. Remove square dish from water; working quickly, swirl melted sugar around bottom and sides of dish to coat. Return dish to water.

Combine eggs, pumpkin, honey, pumpkin pie spice, vanilla and salt in medium bowl. Add evaporated milk; mix well. Pour into prepared square baking dish.

Bake in preheated 350°F. oven for 40 to 45 minutes or until knife inserted near center comes out clean. Remove square baking dish from water. Cool in baking dish on wire rack. Cover and chill for 4 hours or overnight.

To serve, run small spatula around edge of dish. Invert serving plate over baking dish. Invert baking dish; shake gently to release. Cut flan diagonally into quarters; cut each quarter in half to form triangles. Spoon some of the caramel syrup from baking dish over each serving. Garnish with edible nasturtium blossoms, if desired (see tip on edible flowers, *page 11*). Makes 8 servings.

25% lower in fat **FOR LOWER-FAT FLAN:** Use 2 eggs and 2 egg whites in place of the 4 eggs, and CARNATION Evaporated Skimmed Milk in place of the evaporated milk. Prepare and bake as above. Makes 8 servings. Per serving: 1.5 grams fat and 190 calories.

Pumpkin Caramel Flan

Maple Cheesecake

¾ cup graham cracker crumbs

2 tablespoons margarine or butter, melted

1¾ cups (15- or 16-ounce can) LIBBY'S Solid Pack Pumpkin

2 packages (8 ounces *each)* light cream cheese (Neufchâtel)

1 cup packed brown sugar

½ cup part-skim-milk ricotta cheese

2 tablespoons all-purpose flour

1½ teaspoons pumpkin pie spice

1½ teaspoons maple flavoring

½ cup CARNATION Evaporated Skimmed Milk or Evaporated Lowfat Milk

½ cup egg substitute

Maple Topping (recipe follows)

Chopped pecans (optional)

Combine crumbs and margarine in small bowl. Press onto bottom of 9-inch springform pan.

Beat pumpkin, cream cheese, brown sugar, ricotta cheese, flour, pumpkin pie spice and maple flavoring in large mixer bowl on high speed for 1 minute. Beat in evaporated skimmed milk and egg substitute just until blended. Pour over crust.

Bake in preheated 350°F. oven for 65 to 85 minutes or until knife inserted halfway between center and outer edge comes out clean. Remove from oven; cool in pan on wire rack for 10 minutes. Spread with Maple Topping; chill. To serve, remove side of pan and sprinkle with pecans. Makes 16 servings. Per serving: 10 grams fat and 210 calories.

FOR MAPLE TOPPING: Combine ½ cup nonfat sour cream, 1 tablespoon granulated sugar and ¼ teaspoon maple flavoring in small bowl.

Pumpkin Pear Strudel

2 small pears, peeled and diced (about 2 cups)
1 cup LIBBY'S Solid Pack Pumpkin
¾ cup packed brown sugar
¾ cup chopped walnuts
1 teaspoon ground cinnamon
⅛ teaspoon ground cloves

⅛ teaspoon ground ginger
1 package (17¼ ounces) frozen puff pastry, thawed according to package directions (2 sheets)
1 egg, lightly beaten
   Cinnamon Sugar (recipe follows)

Mix pears, pumpkin, brown sugar, walnuts, cinnamon, cloves and ginger in medium bowl. Spoon *half* of the pear mixture down the center ⅓ of 1 pastry sheet. Make downward slanting cuts in outer edges of pastry about ¾ inch apart, cutting from outside edges to within about 1 inch of pear mixture. Starting at top, fold side pastry strips alternately over filling forming chevron design (see photo, *below*). Seal top and bottom ends of strudel. Place on rimmed baking sheet. Repeat with *remaining* pear mixture and *remaining* pastry sheet. Brush both strudels with egg; sprinkle with Cinnamon Sugar.

Bake in preheated 375°F. oven for 25 to 30 minutes or until golden brown and puffy. Cool slightly on baking sheets on wire racks. Serve warm or at room temperature. Makes 10 servings.

FOR CINNAMON SUGAR: Combine ¼ cup granulated sugar and ¾ teaspoon ground cinnamon in a small bowl.

To shape each strudel, starting at the top of the pastry sheet (pastry strips should be slanting down), fold the side pastry strips alternately over the filling to form a chevron design. Seal the top and bottom ends of the strudel.

PUMPKIN ORANGE CAKE ROLL

CAKE ROLL

1 package (16 ounces) angel food cake mix
2½ teaspoons grated orange peel, *divided*
¼ cup powdered sugar

FILLING

1¼ cups LIBBY'S Solid Pack Pumpkin
½ cup granulated sugar
1 teaspoon ground cinnamon
1 teaspoon vanilla extract
   Powdered sugar
2 tablespoons currant or grape jelly (optional)

FOR CAKE ROLL: Prepare cake mix according to package directions, adding *1½ teaspoons* orange peel at end of mixing time. Spread batter evenly into foil-lined 15 x 10-inch jelly-roll pan. (Foil should extend 1 inch above edge of pan.)

Bake at oven temperature suggested in package directions for 30 minutes or until top of cake springs back when touched. While cake is baking, sprinkle towel with powdered sugar. Immediately turn cake out onto towel. Carefully peel off foil. Roll up cake and towel together, starting with a narrow end. Cool on wire rack.

FOR FILLING: Combine pumpkin, granulated sugar, cinnamon, vanilla and *remaining* orange peel in medium bowl.

TO ASSEMBLE: Carefully unroll cake and spread with Filling. Reroll cake. Sprinkle with powdered sugar. Stir jelly well; spoon into small heavy-duty plastic bag. Cut a small hole in corner of bag; squeeze to drizzle jelly over cake roll. Makes 10 servings. Per serving: 0.5 grams fat and 250 calories.

Pumpkin Orange Cake Roll

Pumpkin Mousse Ice-Cream Pie

1¼ cups crushed gingersnap cookies (about 28 cookies)

⅓ cup butter, melted

1 cup granulated sugar, *divided*

2 cups (1 pint) vanilla ice cream

1 cup LIBBY'S Solid Pack Pumpkin

1½ teaspoons pumpkin pie spice

1 cup (8-ounce carton) whipping cream

½ teaspoon vanilla extract

Pumpkin Topping (recipe follows)

Combine crushed gingersnap cookies, butter and ¼ cup sugar in small bowl. Press onto bottom and side of 9-inch pie plate. Bake in preheated 375°F. oven for 8 minutes. Cool on wire rack. Soften ice cream; spread over crust. Freeze until firm.

Combine pumpkin, *remaining* sugar and pumpkin pie spice in medium bowl. Beat whipping cream and vanilla in small mixer bowl until stiff; fold into pumpkin mixture. Spoon over ice cream. Freeze until firm. Serve with Pumpkin Topping. Makes 8 servings.

FOR PUMPKIN TOPPING: Combine 1 jar (12¼ ounces) caramel- or butterscotch-flavored ice-cream topping, ½ cup Libby's Solid Pack Pumpkin and ½ teaspoon pumpkin pie spice in small bowl.

Pumpkin Almond Pie

CRUST
- 1 cup all-purpose flour
- ¼ cup slivered almonds, toasted and finely chopped
- ½ teaspoon salt
- ½ cup shortening
- 2 to 3 tablespoons cold water

PUMPKIN LAYER
- 1 egg
- 1 cup LIBBY'S Solid Pack Pumpkin
- ⅓ cup granulated sugar
- 1 teaspoon pumpkin pie spice

ALMOND LAYER
- ⅔ cup KARO Light Corn Syrup
- 2 eggs
- ½ cup granulated sugar
- 3 tablespoons butter or margarine, melted
- ½ teaspoon almond extract
- 1 cup slivered almonds, toasted

FOR CRUST: Combine flour, almonds and salt in medium bowl; cut in shortening with pastry blender or 2 knives until mixture resembles coarse crumbs. Gradually add water, mixing until ball forms. On lightly floured surface, roll into 12-inch circle. Fit into 9-inch pie plate. Turn under edge; flute.

FOR PUMPKIN LAYER: Combine egg, pumpkin, sugar and pumpkin pie spice in medium bowl. Spread over bottom of the pie shell.

FOR ALMOND LAYER: Combine corn syrup, eggs, sugar, butter and almond extract in medium bowl; stir in almonds. Spoon over pumpkin layer.

Bake in preheated 350°F. oven for 50 to 55 minutes or until filling is set. Cool on wire rack. Makes 8 servings.

CRUMB-TOPPED PUMPKIN PEAR TART

PEAR LAYER
    Pastry for single crust (see recipe, *page 30*)
2 medium-size pears, peeled and thinly sliced
    (about 2 cups)
2 tablespoons granulated sugar
2 teaspoons all-purpose flour
¼ teaspoon ground cinnamon

PUMPKIN LAYER
2 eggs
1½ cups LIBBY'S Solid Pack Pumpkin
1 cup CARNATION Evaporated Milk
½ cup granulated sugar
2 tablespoons butter or margarine, melted
¾ teaspoon ground cinnamon
¼ teaspoon salt
⅛ teaspoon ground nutmeg
    Crumb Topping (recipe follows)

FOR PEAR LAYER: Place pastry in a 10- or 11-inch tart pan with removable bottom (or a 9-inch pie plate). Trim excess pastry.* Combine pears with sugar, flour and cinnamon in medium bowl; place in tart shell.

FOR PUMPKIN LAYER: Combine eggs, pumpkin, evaporated milk, sugar, butter, cinnamon, salt and nutmeg in bowl; pour mixture over pears. Bake in preheated 375°F. oven 25 minutes (30 minutes for pie plate). Remove from oven; sprinkle with Crumb Topping. Bake tart 15 minutes more (20 minutes for pie plate) or until custard is set. Cool. Remove side of tart pan. Makes 10 servings.

FOR CRUMB TOPPING: Combine ½ cup all-purpose flour, ⅓ cup chopped walnuts and 5 tablespoons granulated sugar in medium bowl. Cut in 3 tablespoons softened butter or margarine with pastry blender or 2 knives until crumbly.

*Note: If desired, cut pastry scraps into decorative designs; place on an ungreased baking sheet. Brush with beaten egg. Bake in 375°F. oven 10 minutes or until golden. Place atop baked tart.

Crumb-Topped Pumpkin Pear Tart

Sweet Pie Pleasures

While Libby's Famous Pumpkin Pie has made Libby's a household name, it's just one of many tempting pies that showcase the rich, sweet flavor of pumpkin. Sink your fork into a piece of Pumpkin Dutch Apple Pie or a slice of Macadamia Cheesecake Tart and revel in the perfectly paired flavors. Even the most devoted pumpkin pie fans will delight in this collection of flavorful spin-offs.

Left to right: Pumpkin Dutch Apple Pie (see recipe, page 26) and Macadamia Cheesecake Tart (see recipe, page 27)

Pumpkin Dutch Apple Pie

APPLE LAYER

1 *unbaked* 9-inch (4-cup volume) pie shell with high fluted edge (see recipe, *page 30*)

2 medium-size green apples, peeled and thinly sliced (about 2 cups)

¼ cup granulated sugar

2 teaspoons all-purpose flour

1 teaspoon lemon juice

¼ teaspoon ground cinnamon

PUMPKIN LAYER

2 eggs

1½ cups LIBBY'S Solid Pack Pumpkin

1 cup CARNATION Evaporated Milk

½ cup granulated sugar

2 tablespoons butter or margarine, melted

¾ teaspoon ground cinnamon

¼ teaspoon salt

⅛ teaspoon ground nutmeg

Crumble Topping (recipe follows)

FOR APPLE LAYER: Combine apples with sugar, flour, lemon juice and cinnamon in medium bowl; place in pie shell.

FOR PUMPKIN LAYER: Combine eggs, pumpkin, evaporated milk, sugar, butter, cinnamon, salt and nutmeg in medium bowl; pour over apples.

Bake in preheated 375°F. oven for 30 minutes. Remove from oven; sprinkle with Crumble Topping. Bake for 20 minutes more or until custard is set. Cool on wire rack. Makes 8 servings.

FOR CRUMBLE TOPPING: Combine ½ cup all-purpose flour, ⅓ cup chopped walnuts and 5 tablespoons granulated sugar in medium bowl. Cut in 3 tablespoons softened butter with pastry blender or 2 knives until crumbly.

Pictured on pages 24 and 25.

MACADAMIA CHEESECAKE TART

CRUST
- 1 cup chopped macadamia nuts
- 1 cup quick or old-fashioned oats
- 1 cup flaked coconut
- 2 tablespoons granulated sugar
- 7 tablespoons butter

FILLING
- 1 package (8 ounces) cream cheese, softened
- ½ cup granulated sugar
- 2 eggs
- 1¾ cups (15- or 16-ounce can) LIBBY'S Solid Pack Pumpkin
- 2 teaspoons ground cinnamon
- 1 teaspoon ground ginger
- 1 teaspoon vanilla extract
- Chopped macadamia nuts (optional)
- Toasted coconut (optional)

FOR CRUST: Combine macadamia nuts, oats, coconut and sugar in medium bowl. Cut in butter with pastry blender or 2 knives until blended. Press dough evenly onto bottom and up sides of 11-inch tart pan with removable bottom. Bake in preheated 350°F. oven for 20 to 25 minutes or until lightly browned.

FOR FILLING: Beat cream cheese and sugar in large mixer bowl until well blended. Add eggs, pumpkin, cinnamon, ginger and vanilla; blend well. Pour into baked crust.

Bake at 350°F. for 35 to 40 minutes or until knife inserted near center comes out clean. Cool on wire rack. Chill. Remove side of tart pan. Garnish with additional macadamia nuts and coconut. Makes 14 servings.

Pictured on pages 24 and 25.

Pumpkin Pecan Pie

PUMPKIN LAYER

1 *unbaked* 9-inch (4-cup volume) pie shell (see recipe, *page 30*)
1 egg
1 cup LIBBY'S Solid Pack Pumpkin
⅓ cup granulated sugar
1 teaspoon pumpkin pie spice

PECAN LAYER

⅔ cup KARO Light Corn Syrup
2 eggs
½ cup granulated sugar
3 tablespoons butter or margarine, melted
½ teaspoon vanilla extract
1 cup pecan halves
   Vanilla ice cream (optional)

FOR PUMPKIN LAYER: Combine egg, pumpkin, sugar and pumpkin pie spice in medium bowl. Spread over bottom of pie shell.

FOR PECAN LAYER: Combine corn syrup, eggs, sugar, butter and vanilla in medium bowl; stir in pecans. Spoon over pumpkin layer.

Bake in preheated 350°F. oven for 50 minutes or until filling is set. Cool on wire rack. Serve with ice cream. Makes 8 servings.

PIE-MAKING PERFECTION

Remember these tips from the Libby's Test Kitchen for easy-as-pie success:
- For custard-type pies that call for eggs and milk, use a wire whisk to thoroughly mix the filling ingredients.
- When baking pumpkin and other custard-type pies, start with the higher temperature to help "set" the crust, preventing it from getting soggy. Switch to the lower temperature, allowing the pie to bake gradually and help prevent it from burning.
- Use a glass or dull-finished aluminum pan for a crisper bottom crust. If using a shiny aluminum or foil pan, bake pie on a preheated heavy-duty baking sheet.
- Bake pies one at a time for more even baking. If you need to bake two pies at a time, place them on separate racks, then switch and rotate the pies halfway through baking time.
- If the edge of the crust starts to brown too quickly, cut a 9-inch circle from the center of a square piece of aluminum foil. Carefully place the square piece over the edge of the crust and continue baking until the pie is done.

Pumpkin Pecan Pie

HOMEMADE PASTRY

1 cup all-purpose flour
½ teaspoon salt

6 tablespoons shortening
2 to 3 tablespoons cold water

Mix flour and salt in medium bowl; cut in shortening with pastry blender or 2 knives until crumbly (see photo, *below left*). Gradually stir in cold water, mixing until flour is moistened.

Shape dough into ball; flatten to 1-inch thickness. On lightly floured board, roll dough into a circle about 2 inches larger than inverted 9-inch pie plate. Line pie plate with pastry (see photo, *below center*). Trim pastry to ½ inch beyond the edge of the pie plate; fold extra pastry under and flute edge (see photo, *below right*). Makes one 9-inch pie crust.

Note: Recipe can be doubled to make two 9-inch pie crusts or one double-crust 9-inch pie.

Use a pastry blender or 2 knives to cut in the shortening until mixture is crumbly.

Ease pastry into pie plate, being careful not to stretch pastry.

Trim pastry to ½ inch beyond edge of pie plate; fold under and flute edges.

Sour Cream Orange Pumpkin Pie

1 *unbaked* 9-inch (4-cup volume) pie shell
   (see recipe, *opposite*)
2 eggs
1¾ cups (15- or 16-ounce can) LIBBY'S Solid Pack
   Pumpkin
1¼ cups (14-ounce can) CARNATION Sweetened
   Condensed Milk

1 tablespoon pumpkin pie spice
2 teaspoons grated orange peel
½ teaspoon salt
   Sour Cream Orange Topping (recipe follows)
   Orange slices, cut into wedges (optional)

Combine eggs, pumpkin, sweetened condensed milk, pumpkin pie spice, orange peel and salt in medium bowl; mix well. Pour into prepared pie shell.

Bake in preheated 425°F. oven for 15 minutes. Reduce temperature to 350°F.; bake for 30 to 35 minutes more or until knife inserted near center comes out clean. Cool for 10 minutes on wire rack.

Spread with Sour Cream Orange Topping; bake at 350°F. for 8 minutes more. Cool on wire rack. Garnish with orange wedges. Makes 8 servings.

FOR SOUR CREAM ORANGE TOPPING: Combine 1¼ cups sour cream, 2 tablespoons granulated sugar, 2 teaspoons thawed frozen orange juice concentrate (or orange-flavored liqueur) and ½ teaspoon grated orange peel in small bowl.

Pictured on page 32.

PUMPKIN CHEESECAKE TARTS

⅔ cup finely crushed gingersnap cookies
   (about 12 cookies)
2 tablespoons butter or margarine, melted
1 package (8 ounces) cream cheese, softened
1 cup LIBBY'S Solid Pack Pumpkin
½ cup granulated sugar

1 teaspoon pumpkin pie spice
1 teaspoon vanilla extract
2 eggs
2 tablespoons sour cream (optional)
2 tablespoons NESTLÉ TOLL HOUSE Semi-Sweet
   Chocolate Morsels (optional)

Combine crushed gingersnap cookies and butter in small bowl. Press *scant tablespoon* cookie mixture onto bottom of *each* of 12 paper-lined muffin cups. Bake in preheated 325°F. oven for 5 minutes.

Beat cream cheese, pumpkin, sugar, pumpkin pie spice and vanilla in small mixer bowl until blended. Add eggs; beat well. Pour into muffin cups, filling ¾ full.

Bake at 325°F. for 25 to 30 minutes or until set. Cool in pan on wire rack. Remove tarts from pan; chill.

Garnish with sour cream. Place morsels in small heavy-duty plastic bag. Microwave on HIGH (100%) power for 20 seconds; knead bag to mix. Microwave at additional 10-second intervals, kneading until smooth. Cut a small hole in corner of bag; squeeze to drizzle chocolate over tarts. Makes 1 dozen tarts.

Left to right: Sour Cream Orange Pumpkin Pie
(see recipe, page 31) and Pumpkin Cheesecake Tarts

WALNUT CRUNCH PUMPKIN PIE

1 *unbaked* 9-inch (4-cup volume) pie shell
   (see recipe, *page 30*)
1¼ cups coarsely chopped DIAMOND Walnuts
 ¾ cup packed brown sugar
1¾ cups (15- or 16-ounce can) LIBBY'S Solid Pack
   Pumpkin
1½ cups (12 fluid-ounce can) CARNATION
   Evaporated Milk

¾ cup granulated sugar
2 eggs
1 teaspoon ground cinnamon
½ teaspoon ground ginger
¼ teaspoon salt
¼ teaspoon ground cloves
3 tablespoons butter, melted

Mix walnuts and brown sugar in small bowl; place ¾ *cup* in bottom of pie shell. Reserve remaining mixture for topping. Combine pumpkin, evaporated milk, granulated sugar, eggs, cinnamon, ginger, salt and cloves in large bowl; mix well. Pour into pie shell.

Bake in preheated 425°F. oven for 15 minutes. Reduce temperature to 350°F.; bake for 40 to 50 minutes more or until knife inserted near center comes out clean. Cool on wire rack.

Add butter to *remaining* nut-sugar mixture; stir until moistened. Sprinkle over cooled pie. Broil about 5 inches from heat for 2 to 3 minutes or until bubbly. Cool on wire rack. Makes 8 servings.

Frozen Cranberry Orange Pumpkin Pie

CRUST

1 cup *plus* 2 tablespoons graham cracker crumbs
3 tablespoons butter or margarine, melted
2 tablespoons granulated sugar

FILLING

2 cups (1 pint) orange sherbet, softened
1 cup LIBBY'S Solid Pack Pumpkin
½ teaspoon grated orange peel
1 cup (½ pint) vanilla low-fat or nonfat frozen yogurt
¼ cup chopped cranberries

FOR CRUST: Combine graham cracker crumbs, butter and sugar in medium bowl. Press crumbs onto bottom and up side of 9-inch pie plate. Bake in preheated 375°F. oven for 6 minutes. Cool on wire rack.

FOR FILLING: Combine sherbet, pumpkin and orange peel in medium bowl. Spread evenly over crust; freeze for 2 hours.

Soften frozen yogurt in small bowl. Add cranberries; mix well. Spread mixture over pie; freeze for 2 hours. Makes 8 servings. Per serving: 6 grams fat and 220 calories.

Pumpkin Turnovers

PASTRY

2½ cups all-purpose flour

  2 tablespoons granulated sugar

  1 teaspoon salt

  ½ teaspoon ground cinnamon

  ½ cup (1 stick) butter or margarine, melted

  ½ cup milk

  1 egg

FILLING

1¾ cups (15- or 16-ounce can) LIBBY'S Solid Pack Pumpkin

  ¾ cup packed brown sugar

  ¾ cup chopped pecans or walnuts

  ½ cup raisins

  1 tablespoon lemon juice

  1 tablespoon water

  1 teaspoon ground cinnamon

  ⅛ teaspoon ground cloves

  1 egg, lightly beaten

  Cinnamon Sugar (recipe follows)

FOR PASTRY: Combine flour, granulated sugar, salt and cinnamon in medium bowl. Beat butter, milk and egg in small bowl until combined. Add to flour mixture; mix well. Form into ball. Cover; chill for 1 hour.

FOR FILLING: Combine pumpkin and brown sugar in medium bowl. Add pecans, raisins, lemon juice, water, cinnamon and cloves; mix well.

Divide pastry into 12 to 14 portions. On lightly floured board, roll *each* portion into 6-inch circle. Place *scant ¼ cup* filling on *each* circle. Moisten edges with water; fold in half, pressing edges with fork to seal. Scallop sealed edges by indenting with handle of fork at ¾-inch intervals. Place on ungreased baking sheet. Brush egg over tops of turnovers. Sprinkle with Cinnamon Sugar.

Bake in preheated 400°F. oven for 15 to 20 minutes or until golden brown. Serve warm, or cool on wire rack. Makes 12 to 14.

FOR CINNAMON SUGAR: Combine ¼ cup granulated sugar and 1 teaspoon ground cinnamon in small bowl.

Pumpkin Turnovers

PEANUT BUTTER PUMPKIN PIE

1 *unbaked* 9-inch (4-cup volume) pie shell
   (see recipe, *page 28*)
1¾ cups (15- or 16-ounce can) LIBBY'S Solid Pack
   Pumpkin
1 cup CARNATION Evaporated Milk
¾ cup packed brown sugar

3 eggs
½ cup creamy peanut butter
½ teaspoon pumpkin pie spice
¼ teaspoon salt
   Whipped cream (optional)
   Chopped peanuts (optional)

Combine pumpkin, evaporated milk, brown sugar, eggs, peanut butter, pumpkin pie spice and salt in large bowl. Pour into pie shell.

Bake in preheated 425°F. oven for 15 minutes. Reduce temperature to 350°F.; bake for 40 to 45 minutes more or until knife inserted near center comes out clean. Cool on wire rack. Garnish with whipped cream and peanuts. Makes 8 servings.

WHAT TO DO WITH EXTRA PUMPKIN

If your recipe calls for less than a whole can of pumpkin (approximately 1¾ cups), save the rest and try one of the quick-fix ideas below. Before storing, always transfer the pumpkin from the can to an airtight container or zip-top plastic bag. Store leftover pumpkin in the refrigerator for 1 week or in the freezer for up to 3 months.

- Whisk pumpkin into soups and sauces. You'll add flavor and nutrients.
- Stir pumpkin into mashed potatoes for a festive, fall-color favorite.
- Create a sauce for pancakes, waffles or ice cream by mixing pumpkin with maple syrup, brown sugar or honey and cinnamon (see recipe, *page 78*).
- Stir pumpkin into softened ice cream (try vanilla, caramel swirl or butter pecan flavors) for a quick, new dessert idea.
- Mix pumpkin with prepared (and partially set-up) vanilla or butterscotch pudding. For a fast and easy fat-free treat, use fat-free pudding made with nonfat milk and pumpkin.

Pumpkin Apricot Crumble Pie

1 *unbaked* 9-inch (4-cup volume) pie shell (see recipe, *page 30*)
¾ cup finely chopped dried apricots
¾ cup coarsely chopped walnuts
¾ cup packed brown sugar
1¾ cups (15- or 16-ounce can) LIBBY'S Solid Pack Pumpkin
1¼ cups CARNATION Evaporated Milk

2 eggs
½ cup granulated sugar
¼ cup apricot preserves
1 teaspoon ground cinnamon
1 teaspoon ground ginger
¼ teaspoon salt
¼ teaspoon ground cloves
3 tablespoons butter, melted

Mix apricots, walnuts and brown sugar in small bowl; place ¾ *cup* in bottom of pie shell. Reserve remaining mixture for topping. Combine pumpkin, evaporated milk, eggs, granulated sugar, apricot preserves, cinnamon, ginger, salt and cloves in large bowl; mix well. Pour into pie shell.

Bake in preheated 425°F. oven for 15 minutes. Reduce temperature to 350°F.; bake for 40 to 50 minutes more or until knife inserted near center comes out clean. Cool on wire rack.

Add butter to remaining apricot mixture; stir until moistened. Sprinkle over cooled pie. Broil about 5 inches from heat for 2 to 3 minutes or until bubbly. Cool on wire rack. Makes 8 servings.

CLASSIC CAKES

Some cake recipes pass from generation to generation, winning the hearts of many. From cheesecakes to coffeecakes, these classic recipes call for the same ingredients that our grandmas and moms used for baking, with equally wonderful results.

Clockwise from top right: White Chip Spice Cake
(see recipe, page 42), Pumpkin Cheesecake (see recipe, page 43)
and Quick Pumpkin Cupcakes (see recipe, page 48)

WHITE CHIP SPICE CAKE

1 package (18¼ ounces) spice cake mix
1 cup LIBBY'S Solid Pack Pumpkin
3 eggs
⅔ cup CARNATION Evaporated Milk, *divided*

⅓ cup vegetable oil
2 cups (12-ounce package) NESTLÉ TOLL HOUSE Premier White Morsels, *divided*
½ teaspoon ground cinnamon

Beat cake mix, pumpkin, eggs, *⅓ cup* evaporated milk and vegetable oil in large mixer bowl on low speed until moistened. Beat on medium speed for 2 minutes; stir in *1 cup* morsels. Pour into greased and floured 12-cup fluted tube pan.

Bake in preheated 350°F. oven for 40 to 45 minutes or until wooden pick inserted in cake comes out clean. Cool in pan on wire rack 25 minutes. Invert onto wire rack to cool completely.

Heat *remaining* evaporated milk in small, heavy saucepan over medium heat just to a boil; remove from heat. Add *remaining* morsels, stirring until smooth and melted. Stir in cinnamon. Drizzle some of the mixture over cake; serve cake with remaining mixture. Makes 18 servings.

Pictured on pages 40 and 41.

CHEESECAKE SUCCESS

Cheesecakes need a little special care for picture-perfect results. Count on these tips for sweet success:
- Use a springform pan with removable side and bottom for best results.
- For cheesecakes with a crumb crust, spray bottom and side lightly with no-stick spray before adding the crumbs. This helps them stick to the pan.
- Use cream cheese that is at room temperature, but not too soft. To avoid lumps in your cheesecake, make sure the cream cheese and sugar are thoroughly combined before adding the other ingredients.
- To help prevent cracking after the cake is baked, be careful not to overbeat the batter, especially after the eggs have been added.
- Wrap cooled cheesecake with plastic wrap and store in the refrigerator.

Pumpkin Cheesecake

CRUST

1½ cups graham cracker crumbs

⅓ cup butter or margarine, melted

¼ cup granulated sugar

CHEESECAKE

3 packages (8 ounces *each*) cream cheese, softened

1 cup granulated sugar

¼ cup packed brown sugar

1¾ cups (15- or 16-ounce can) LIBBY'S Solid Pack Pumpkin

2 eggs

⅔ cup CARNATION Evaporated Milk

2 tablespoons cornstarch

1¼ teaspoons ground cinnamon

½ teaspoon ground nutmeg

TOPPING

2 cups (16-ounce carton) sour cream, at room temperature

¼ to ⅓ cup granulated sugar

1 teaspoon vanilla extract

Whole strawberries, sliced and fanned (optional)

FOR CRUST: Combine graham cracker crumbs, butter and granulated sugar in medium bowl. Press onto bottom and 1 inch up side of 9-inch springform pan. Bake in preheated 350°F. oven for 6 to 8 minutes. Do not allow to brown. Cool on wire rack.

FOR CHEESECAKE: Beat cream cheese, granulated sugar and brown sugar in large mixer bowl until fluffy. Beat in pumpkin, eggs and evaporated milk. Add cornstarch, cinnamon and nutmeg; beat well. Pour into crust.

Bake at 350°F. for 55 to 60 minutes or until edge is set but center still moves slightly.

FOR TOPPING: Combine sour cream, granulated sugar and vanilla in small bowl. Spread over surface of warm cheesecake. Bake at 350°F. for 8 minutes more. Cool in pan on wire rack. Chill for several hours or overnight; remove side of pan. Garnish with strawberries. Makes 16 servings.

Pictured on pages 40 and 41.

PUMPKIN CARROT CAKE

2 cups all-purpose flour
2 teaspoons baking soda
2 teaspoons ground cinnamon
½ teaspoon salt
¾ cup milk
1½ teaspoons lemon juice
1½ cups granulated sugar
1¼ cups LIBBY'S Solid Pack Pumpkin

3 eggs
½ cup packed brown sugar
½ cup vegetable oil
1 cup (8-ounce can) crushed pineapple, drained
1 cup grated carrots (about 3 medium)
1 cup flaked coconut
1¼ cups chopped DIAMOND Walnuts, *divided*
    Cream Cheese Frosting (recipe follows)

Combine flour, baking soda, cinnamon and salt in small bowl. Combine milk and lemon juice in liquid measuring cup (mixture will appear curdled).

Beat granulated sugar, pumpkin, eggs, brown sugar and vegetable oil in large mixer bowl until combined. Beat in pineapple, carrots and milk mixture until combined. Gradually beat in flour mixture. Stir in coconut and *1 cup* walnuts. Pour into 2 greased 9-inch round cake pans.

Bake in preheated 350°F. oven for 30 to 35 minutes or until wooden pick inserted in center comes out clean. Cool in pans on wire racks for 15 minutes. Remove to racks to cool completely.

TO ASSEMBLE: Frost between layers, on side and top of cake with Cream Cheese Frosting. Garnish side of cake with *remaining* walnuts. Store in refrigerator. Makes 12 servings.

FOR CREAM CHEESE FROSTING: Beat 1 package (8 ounces) *and* 1 package (3 ounces) softened cream cheese and ⅓ cup softened butter in large mixer bowl; gradually beat in 3½ cups sifted powdered sugar. Beat in 2 teaspoons orange juice, 1 teaspoon vanilla extract and 1 teaspoon grated orange peel until fluffy.

Pumpkin Carrot Cake

PUMPKIN STREUSEL COFFEECAKE

STREUSEL TOPPING
- ½ cup all-purpose flour
- ¼ cup packed brown sugar
- 1½ teaspoons ground cinnamon
- 3 tablespoons butter or margarine
- ½ cup coarsely chopped nuts

COFFEECAKE
- 2 cups all-purpose flour
- 2 teaspoons baking powder
- 1½ teaspoons ground cinnamon
- ½ teaspoon baking soda
- ¼ teaspoon salt
- 1 cup (2 sticks) butter or margarine, softened
- 1 cup granulated sugar
- 2 eggs
- 1 cup LIBBY'S Solid Pack Pumpkin
- 1 teaspoon vanilla extract

FOR STREUSEL TOPPING: Combine flour, brown sugar and cinnamon in medium bowl. Cut in butter with pastry blender or 2 knives until mixture is crumbly; stir in nuts.

FOR COFFEECAKE: Combine flour, baking powder, cinnamon, baking soda and salt in small bowl. Beat butter and granulated sugar in large mixer bowl until creamy. Add eggs 1 at a time, beating well after each addition. Beat in pumpkin and vanilla. Gradually beat in flour mixture.

Spoon *half* of batter into greased and floured 9-inch round cake pan. Sprinkle ¾ *cup* Streusel Topping over batter. Spoon *remaining* batter evenly over Streusel Topping; sprinkle with *remaining* Streusel Topping.

Bake in preheated 350°F. oven for 45 to 50 minutes or until wooden pick inserted in center comes out clean. Cool in pan on wire rack for 15 minutes; serve warm. Makes 10 servings.

Pumpkin Streusel Coffeecake

Quick Pumpkin Cupcakes

1 package (16 ounces) pound cake mix
1 cup LIBBY'S Solid Pack Pumpkin
2 eggs
⅓ cup water

2 teaspoons pumpkin pie spice
1 teaspoon baking soda
1 container (16 ounces) prepared vanilla frosting
   Walnut halves (optional)

Beat cake mix, pumpkin, eggs, water, pumpkin pie spice and baking soda in large mixer bowl on medium speed for 3 minutes. Pour batter into 12 to 14 paper-lined muffin cups.

Bake in preheated 325°F. oven for 25 to 30 minutes or until golden brown. Cool in pan on wire rack for 10 minutes. Remove to wire rack to cool completely. Spread cupcakes with frosting. Top with walnut halves. Makes 12 to 14 cupcakes.

Pictured on pages 40 and 41.

SOUR CREAM PUMPKIN COFFEECAKE

STREUSEL

½ cup packed brown sugar
1 teaspoon ground cinnamon
¼ teaspoon ground allspice
2 teaspoons butter or margarine

BATTER

3 cups all-purpose flour
1 tablespoon ground cinnamon
2 teaspoons baking soda
1 teaspoon salt
1 cup (2 sticks) butter or margarine, softened
2 cups granulated sugar
4 eggs
1 cup LIBBY'S Solid Pack Pumpkin
1 cup sour cream
2 teaspoons vanilla extract

FOR STREUSEL: Combine brown sugar, cinnamon and allspice in small bowl. Cut in butter with pastry blender or 2 knives until mixture is crumbly.

FOR BATTER: Combine flour, cinnamon, baking soda and salt in medium bowl. Beat butter and granulated sugar in large mixer bowl until light and fluffy. Beat in eggs 1 at a time, beating well after each addition.

Beat in pumpkin, sour cream and vanilla. Gradually beat in the flour mixture.

Spoon *half* of the batter into a greased 12-cup fluted tube pan. Sprinkle Streusel over batter, making sure Streusel *does not* touch side of pan. Top with *remaining* batter, making sure batter layer touches side of pan. Bake in preheated 350°F. oven for 55 to 60 minutes or until wooden pick comes out clean. Cool in pan on rack for 30 minutes. Invert onto rack to cool. Makes 16 servings.

TOFFEE CHEESECAKE

CRUST

1¾ cups finely crushed toffee shortbread cookies (about 14 to 16 cookies)

4 teaspoons butter or margarine, melted

CHEESECAKE

3 packages (8 ounces *each)* cream cheese, softened

1¼ cups packed brown sugar

1¾ cups (15- or 16-ounce can) LIBBY'S Solid Pack Pumpkin

2 eggs

⅔ cup CARNATION Evaporated Milk

2 tablespoons cornstarch

½ teaspoon ground cinnamon

⅔ cup chopped or crushed toffee candies (about 24 candies), *divided*

TOPPING

2 cups (16-ounce carton) sour cream, at room temperature

¼ cup granulated sugar

½ teaspoon vanilla extract

Caramel-flavored ice-cream topping (optional)

FOR CRUST: Combine crushed cookies and butter in small bowl. Press onto bottom and 1 inch up side of 9-inch springform pan. Bake in preheated 350°F. oven for 6 to 8 minutes. Do not allow to brown. Cool on wire rack.

FOR CHEESECAKE: Beat cream cheese and brown sugar in large mixer bowl on medium speed until creamy. Beat in pumpkin, eggs, evaporated milk, cornstarch and cinnamon. Stir in ⅓ *cup* toffee pieces. Pour into prepared crust.

Bake at 350°F. for 60 to 65 minutes or until edge is set but center still moves slightly.

FOR TOPPING: Combine sour cream, granulated sugar, vanilla and *remaining* toffee pieces in small bowl. Spread over surface of warm cheesecake. Bake at 350°F. for 8 minutes more. Cool in pan on wire rack. Chill several hours or overnight; remove side of pan. Before serving, drizzle with caramel topping, if desired. Makes 16 servings.

Toffee Cheesecake

PUMPKIN ORANGE CHEESECAKE

CRUST
 ¾ cup graham cracker crumbs
 2 tablespoons margarine or butter, melted

FILLING
 2 packages (8 ounces *each*) light cream cheese
   (Neufchâtel), softened
 ¾ cup packed brown sugar
 ½ cup nonfat ricotta cheese

1½ cups LIBBY'S Solid Pack Pumpkin
 3 tablespoons orange juice
 2 tablespoons CARNATION Evaporated Skimmed Milk
 2 teaspoons vanilla extract
1½ teaspoons pumpkin pie spice
 1 teaspoon grated orange peel
 ¾ cup frozen egg substitute, thawed
   Orange Topping (recipe follows)

FOR CRUST: Combine graham cracker crumbs and margarine in small bowl. Press onto bottom of 9-inch springform pan.

FOR FILLING: Beat cream cheese, brown sugar and ricotta cheese in large mixer bowl until fluffy. Add pumpkin, orange juice, evaporated skimmed milk, vanilla, pumpkin pie spice and orange peel; beat until well blended. Add egg substitute and beat just until blended. Pour into prepared crust.

Bake in preheated 350°F. oven for 60 to 65 minutes or until edge is set but center still moves slightly. Cool in pan on wire rack; spread with Orange Topping. Chill several hours or overnight; remove side of pan. Makes 12 servings. Per serving: 5 grams fat and 200 calories.

FOR ORANGE TOPPING: Combine ½ cup light sour cream, 1 tablespoon granulated sugar and 1 teaspoon orange juice.

Pumpkin White Chunk Cake

3 cups buttermilk baking mix
1½ cups granulated sugar
2½ teaspoons ground cinnamon
1 cup LIBBY'S Solid Pack Pumpkin
2 eggs, lightly beaten
½ cup water

2 teaspoons vanilla extract
3 bars (one 6-ounce package) NESTLÉ TOLL HOUSE Premier White Baking Bars, coarsely chopped, *divided*
⅔ cup chopped pecans, *divided*

Stir together baking mix, sugar and cinnamon in large bowl. Stir in pumpkin, eggs, water and vanilla just until moistened. Stir in *half* of baking bars and *half* of pecans. Spread into greased 13 x 9-inch baking pan.

Bake in preheated 350°F. oven for 20 minutes. Sprinkle with *remaining* baking bars and *remaining* pecans. Bake for 10 to 15 minutes more or until wooden pick inserted in center comes out clean. Cool completely in pan on wire rack. Makes 16 servings.

FAMILY-FAVORITE COOKIES

Lions and tigers and bears, oh yes! A little frosting turns Great Pumpkin Cookies into whimsical zoo animals sure to bring smiles and giggles. Gather the whole family to share in the cookie-baking fun, then offer a plateful of homemade cookies or bars as their just reward.

Great Pumpkin Cookies
(see recipe, page 56)

GREAT PUMPKIN COOKIES

2 cups all-purpose flour
1⅓ cups quick or old-fashioned oats
1 teaspoon baking soda
1 teaspoon ground cinnamon
½ teaspoon salt
1 cup (2 sticks) butter or margarine, softened
1 cup granulated sugar
1 cup packed brown sugar

1 cup LIBBY'S Solid Pack Pumpkin
1 egg
1 teaspoon vanilla extract
¾ cup chopped nuts
¾ cup raisins
Colored icings in tubes
NESTLÉ TOLL HOUSE Semi-Sweet Chocolate Morsels
Assorted candies

Combine flour, oats, baking soda, cinnamon and salt in medium bowl. Beat butter, granulated sugar and brown sugar in large mixer bowl until creamy. Beat in pumpkin, egg and vanilla until well mixed. Gradually beat in flour mixture. Stir in nuts and raisins. For *each* cookie, drop about ¼ *cup* dough onto greased baking sheet; spread dough into round, triangular or oval shapes about 3 inches across.

Bake in preheated 350°F. oven for 14 to 16 minutes or until cookies are firm and lightly browned. Let stand for 2 minutes; remove to wire racks to cool completely. Decorate with icing, morsels and assorted candies. Makes about 20 large cookies.

Pictured on pages 54 and 55.

COOKIE DECORATING TIPS

Put on your artist's cap and use cookies as your canvas. These designer tips will help you get started.
- Always cool baked cookies before decorating with icing and candies.
- For colored frosting, tint vanilla frosting with food coloring. Use paste food coloring for more vibrant colors, starting with a small amount, then adding more as needed.
- To decorate cookies with frosting, try a pastry bag with tips, purchased frosting in tubes or a plastic bag with a corner snipped off. If spreading frosting with a knife, thin frosting with milk to desired consistency.
- Top cookies with candy sprinkles, cinnamon red hots, chopped nuts, NESTLÉ TOLL HOUSE Morsels, raisins, candy corn, licorice or coconut.

BUTTERSCOTCH FUDGE SQUARES

COOKIE BASE

- 1 cup all-purpose flour
- 1 cup quick or old-fashioned oats
- ¾ cup packed brown sugar
- ½ cup chopped DIAMOND Walnuts
- ½ cup flaked coconut
- ¾ teaspoon pumpkin pie spice
- ½ teaspoon baking soda
- ¾ cup (1½ sticks) butter or margarine, melted

FUDGE

- 1½ cups granulated sugar
- ⅔ cup CARNATION Evaporated Milk
- ½ cup LIBBY'S Solid Pack Pumpkin
- 2 tablespoons butter or margarine
- 1½ teaspoons pumpkin pie spice
- ¼ teaspoon salt
- 2 cups (4 ounces) mini marshmallows
- 2 cups (12-ounce package) NESTLÉ TOLL HOUSE Butterscotch Flavored Morsels
- ¾ cup chopped DIAMOND Walnuts, *divided*
- 1 teaspoon vanilla extract

FOR COOKIE BASE: Combine flour, oats, brown sugar, walnuts, coconut, pumpkin pie spice and baking soda in medium bowl. Stir in melted butter, mixing well. Press into foil-lined 15 x 10-inch jelly-roll pan. Bake in preheated 350°F. oven for 13 to 15 minutes or until slightly brown. Cool in pan on wire rack.

FOR FUDGE: Combine granulated sugar, evaporated milk, pumpkin, butter, pumpkin pie spice and salt in medium, heavy saucepan. Bring to a boil over medium heat, stirring constantly. Boil for 8 to 10 minutes, stirring constantly. Remove from heat.

Stir in marshmallows, morsels, *½ cup* walnuts and vanilla. Stir vigorously for 1 minute or until marshmallows are melted. Pour over cooled cookie base; sprinkle with *remaining* walnuts. Chill until firm. Cut into squares. Makes 4 dozen squares.

Pictured on page 59.

PUMPKIN CARROT SWIRL BARS

2 cups all-purpose flour
2¼ teaspoons pumpkin pie spice
2 teaspoons baking powder
1 teaspoon baking soda
⅓ cup butter or margarine, softened
1 cup granulated sugar
½ cup packed brown sugar

1¾ cups (15- or 16-ounce can) LIBBY'S Solid Pack Pumpkin
1 cup finely shredded carrots
2 eggs
2 egg whites
Cream Cheese Topping (recipe follows)

Combine flour, pumpkin pie spice, baking powder and baking soda in small bowl.

Beat butter, granulated sugar and brown sugar in large mixer bowl until crumbly. Beat in pumpkin, carrots, eggs and egg whites until well mixed. Gradually beat in flour mixture. Spread into greased 15 x 10-inch jelly-roll pan. Dollop with teaspoonfuls of Cream Cheese Topping; swirl with spoon to marbleize.

Bake in preheated 350°F. oven for 25 to 30 minutes or until wooden pick inserted in center comes out clean. Cool completely in pan on wire rack. Cut into bars. Makes 4 dozen bars. Per bar: 3 grams fat and 80 calories.

FOR CREAM CHEESE TOPPING: Beat 4 ounces softened light cream cheese (Neufchâtel), ¼ cup granulated sugar and 1 tablespoon milk in small mixer bowl until combined.

Clockwise from top right: Pumpkin Carrot Swirl Bars, Butterscotch Fudge Squares (see recipe, page 57) and Pumpkin Layer Bars (see recipe, page 60)

Pumpkin Layer Bars

¾ cup all-purpose flour

⅓ cup packed brown sugar

⅓ cup quick or old-fashioned oats

¼ cup chopped nuts

1½ teaspoons ground cinnamon

⅓ cup butter or margarine, melted

1¼ cups LIBBY'S Solid Pack Pumpkin

1 cup CARNATION Evaporated Milk

½ cup granulated sugar

1 egg

¾ teaspoon pumpkin pie spice

¼ teaspoon salt

4 ounces cream cheese, softened

¼ cup sour cream, at room temperature

2 tablespoons orange marmalade

Combine flour, brown sugar, oats, nuts and cinnamon in medium bowl. Stir in butter, mixing well. Press onto bottom of 9-inch square baking pan. Bake in preheated 350°F. oven for 20 to 25 minutes or until golden brown. Remove from oven.

Combine pumpkin, evaporated milk, granulated sugar, egg, pumpkin pie spice and salt in medium bowl. Pour over oat mixture; bake at 350°F. for 20 to 25 minutes or until knife inserted near center comes out clean. Cool in pan on wire rack.

Combine cream cheese and sour cream in small bowl. Stir in orange marmalade. Spread over pumpkin layer. Chill. Cut into bars. Makes 2 dozen bars.

Pictured on page 59.

Sour Cream Walnut Bars

2 cups all-purpose flour
2 teaspoons ground cinnamon
1 teaspoon baking powder
1 teaspoon baking soda
1 teaspoon ground ginger
¾ teaspoon salt
½ teaspoon ground allspice
1½ cups granulated sugar

1 cup sour cream
½ cup (1 stick) butter or margarine, softened
2 eggs
1 cup LIBBY'S Solid Pack Pumpkin
2 teaspoons vanilla extract
½ cup chopped nuts
Butter Icing (recipe follows)

Combine flour, cinnamon, baking powder, baking soda, ginger, salt and allspice in medium bowl. Beat sugar, sour cream, butter and eggs in large mixer bowl until blended. Beat in pumpkin and vanilla. Gradually beat in flour mixture. Stir in nuts. Spread batter into greased and floured 15 x 10-inch jelly-roll pan.

Bake in preheated 375°F. oven for 20 to 25 minutes or until wooden pick inserted in center comes out clean. Cool completely in pan on wire rack; spread with Butter Icing. Cut into bars. Makes 4 dozen bars.

FOR BUTTER ICING: Heat ⅓ cup butter in medium saucepan over medium heat, stirring until melted; remove from heat. Stir in 3 cups sifted powdered sugar and 1 teaspoon vanilla extract. Stir in 4 to 6 tablespoons milk until icing is of spreading consistency.

MACADAMIA NUT
WHITE CHIP COOKIES

2 cups all-purpose flour
2 teaspoons ground cinnamon
1 teaspoon ground cardamom
1 teaspoon baking soda
1 cup (2 sticks) butter or margarine, softened
½ cup granulated sugar
½ cup packed brown sugar

1 cup LIBBY'S Solid Pack Pumpkin
1 egg
2 teaspoons vanilla extract
2 cups (12-ounce package) NESTLÉ TOLL HOUSE Premier White Morsels
⅔ cup coarsely chopped macadamia nuts, toasted

Combine flour, cinnamon, cardamom and baking soda in small bowl. Beat butter, granulated sugar and brown sugar in large mixer bowl until creamy. Beat in pumpkin, egg and vanilla until well mixed. Gradually beat in flour mixture. Stir in morsels and macadamia nuts.

Drop by rounded tablespoon onto greased baking sheets; flatten with back of spoon or greased bottom of glass dipped in sugar.

Bake in preheated 350°F. oven for 11 to 14 minutes or until edges are set. Cool for 2 minutes; remove to wire racks to cool completely. Makes about 4 dozen cookies.

Top to bottom: Macadamia Nut White Chip Cookies and Pumpkin Orange Cookies
(see recipe, page 64)

PUMPKIN ORANGE COOKIES

2½ cups all-purpose flour
½ teaspoon baking soda
½ teaspoon salt
1 cup (2 sticks) butter or margarine
1 cup granulated sugar
½ cup packed brown sugar

1¼ cups LIBBY'S Solid Pack Pumpkin
1 egg
2 tablespoons orange juice
1 teaspoon grated orange peel
½ cup chopped nuts (optional)
Orange Icing (recipe follows)

Combine flour, baking soda and salt in medium bowl. Beat butter, granulated sugar and brown sugar in large mixer bowl until creamy. Beat in pumpkin, egg, orange juice and orange peel until combined. Gradually beat in flour mixture. Stir in nuts.

Drop dough by rounded tablespoon onto ungreased baking sheets. Bake in preheated 375°F. oven for 12 to 14 minutes or until edges are set. Remove cookies immediately to wire rack to cool completely. Spread cookies with Orange Icing. Makes about 4 dozen cookies.

FOR ORANGE ICING: Combine 1½ cups sifted powdered sugar, ½ teaspoon grated orange peel and enough orange juice until of desired consistency (1 to 3 tablespoons) in medium bowl. Stir until smooth.

Pictured on page 63.

Iced Pumpkin Blondies

2¼ cups all-purpose flour
2½ teaspoons baking powder
2 teaspoons ground cinnamon
¼ teaspoon salt
¾ cup (1½ sticks) butter or margarine, softened

1½ cups packed brown sugar
1 teaspoon vanilla extract
2 eggs
1 cup LIBBY'S Solid Pack Pumpkin
Maple Icing (recipe follows)

Combine flour, baking powder, cinnamon and salt in medium bowl. Beat butter, brown sugar and vanilla in large mixer bowl until creamy. Add eggs 1 at a time, beating well after each addition. Beat in pumpkin. Gradually beat in flour mixture. Spread into greased 15 x 10-inch jelly-roll pan.

Bake in preheated 350°F. oven for 20 to 25 minutes or until wooden pick inserted in center comes out clean. Cool completely in pan on wire rack; spread with Maple Icing. Cut into bars. Makes 4 dozen bars.

FOR MAPLE ICING: Beat 2 packages (3 ounces *each*) softened cream cheese and 2 tablespoons softened butter or margarine in small mixer bowl; gradually beat in 2 cups sifted powdered sugar. Beat in 1 to 2 teaspoons maple flavoring until fluffy.

Hearth-to-Heart Breads

A loaf of bread baking, with its soul-soothing aroma, draws everyone to the kitchen in anticipation. Treat loved ones to a round of gooey cinnamon rolls or a loaf of hearty pumpkin bread. This baker's dozen of recipes offers breads, rolls and other baked goods, just right for mealtime or midday snacking.

Left to right: Pumpkin Swirl Breakfast Rolls (see recipe, page 68) and Pumpkin Honey Wheat Bread (see recipe, page 69)

Pumpkin Swirl Breakfast Rolls

½ cup packed brown sugar
¾ teaspoon ground cinnamon
⅛ teaspoon ground cloves
⅓ cup butter or margarine
1 cup LIBBY'S Solid Pack Pumpkin

¾ cup chopped walnuts or pecans
⅓ cup raisins
1 pound frozen bread dough, thawed
Glaze (recipe follows)

Combine brown sugar, cinnamon and cloves in medium bowl. Cut in butter with a pastry blender or 2 knives until crumbly. Stir in pumpkin, walnuts, and raisins.

Roll bread dough into 12 x 12-inch square;* spread with pumpkin mixture, leaving 1-inch border along 2 sides. Roll up dough, starting from side with 1-inch border; seal edges. Slice into 12 pieces; place cut side up in greased 9-inch round or square baking pan. Let rise in warm place until double in size.

Bake in preheated 375°F. oven for 20 to 25 minutes or until golden brown. Cool slightly on wire rack. Drizzle with Glaze. Serve warm. Makes 1 dozen rolls.

FOR GLAZE: Combine 1 cup sifted powdered sugar and 2 to 3 tablespoons water in small bowl until smooth.

*Note: For extra large rolls, roll dough into 12 x 9-inch rectangle. Spread with pumpkin mixure, leaving 1-inch border along 9-inch sides. Roll up dough, starting from 9-inch side; seal edges. Slice into 6 pieces; place cut side up in greased 9-inch baking pan. Let rise and bake as above. Makes 6 rolls.

Pictured on the cover and pages 66 and 67.

Pumpkin Honey Wheat Bread

2¼ cups all-purpose flour
¾ cup wheat germ
2½ teaspoons baking powder
1½ teaspoons ground cinnamon
1 teaspoon salt
½ teaspoon baking soda

1¼ cups LIBBY'S Solid Pack Pumpkin
¾ cup honey
2 eggs
¼ cup vegetable oil
¼ cup milk
¼ cup pine nuts or sunflower seeds

Combine flour, wheat germ, baking powder, cinnamon, salt and baking soda in large bowl. Combine pumpkin, honey, eggs, vegetable oil and milk in medium bowl; add to flour mixture. Stir just until blended.

Spread batter into greased 9 x 5-inch loaf pan. Sprinkle with pine nuts; gently pat into batter. Bake in preheated 350°F. oven for 55 to 60 minutes or until wooden pick inserted in center comes out clean. Cool in pan on wire rack for 10 minutes; remove to wire rack to cool completely. Makes 1 loaf.

Pictured on pages 66 and 67.

Pumpkin Apricot Muffins

1⅔ cups all-purpose flour
1 tablespoon baking powder
¾ teaspoon ground cinnamon
¼ teaspoon salt
1 cup LIBBY'S Solid Pack Pumpkin
¾ cup milk

2 eggs
½ cup packed brown sugar
½ cup dried apricots, chopped
¼ cup (½ stick) butter or margarine, melted
  Streusel Topping (recipe follows)

Combine flour, baking powder, cinnamon and salt in medium bowl. Mix pumpkin, milk, eggs, brown sugar, apricots and butter in small bowl; add to flour mixture and stir just until moistened. Spoon into 12 greased or paper-lined muffin cups. Sprinkle with Streusel Topping. Bake in preheated 375°F. oven for 20 to 25 minutes or until wooden pick inserted in center comes out clean. Remove to wire rack; cool slightly. Serve warm. Makes 1 dozen.

FOR STREUSEL TOPPING: Combine 3 tablespoons finely chopped walnuts, 2 tablespoons granulated sugar and ⅛ teaspoon ground cinnamon in small bowl.

Pumpkin Corn Muffins

1¼ cups all-purpose flour
1 cup cornmeal
⅓ cup granulated sugar
4 teaspoons baking powder
½ teaspoon salt

1¼ cups LIBBY'S Solid Pack Pumpkin
2 eggs
⅓ cup milk
¼ cup vegetable oil

Combine flour, cornmeal, sugar, baking powder and salt in large bowl. Beat pumpkin, eggs, milk and vegetable oil in medium bowl. Add to flour mixture; mix well. Spoon into 12 greased or paper-lined muffin cups. Bake in preheated 375°F. oven 25 to 30 minutes or until wooden pick inserted in center comes out clean. Remove to wire rack; cool slightly. Serve warm. Makes 1 dozen.

Left to right: Pumpkin Apricot Muffins and Pumpkin Corn Muffins

PUMPKIN SCONES

2½ cups all-purpose flour
¼ cup packed brown sugar
1 tablespoon baking powder
1 teaspoon ground cinnamon
½ teaspoon salt

¼ teaspoon ground cloves
½ cup shortening
¾ cup LIBBY'S Solid Pack Pumpkin
½ cup milk

Combine flour, brown sugar, baking powder, cinnamon, salt and cloves in large bowl. Cut in shortening with pastry blender or 2 knives until mixture resembles coarse crumbs. Combine pumpkin and milk in small bowl. Add to flour mixture; mix just until dough forms.

Knead dough gently on floured surface 10 to 12 times. Pat *half* of dough into one 7-inch circle; cut into 6 to 8 wedges. Repeat with *remaining* dough. Place wedges 2 inches apart on ungreased baking sheet.

Bake in preheated 450°F. oven for 12 to 14 minutes or until light golden color. Remove scones to wire rack; cool slightly. Serve warm. Makes 12 to 16 scones.

Pumpkin Scones (see recipe, opposite) and Pumpkin Apple Butter

PUMPKIN APPLE BUTTER

1¾ cups (15- or 16-ounce can) LIBBY'S Solid Pack
     Pumpkin
 1 cup apple juice

1 cup peeled and grated apple (about 1 medium)
½ cup packed brown sugar
¾ teaspoon pumpkin pie spice

Combine pumpkin, apple juice, apple, brown sugar and pumpkin pie spice in 2-quart saucepan. Bring to a boil; reduce heat. Simmer, uncovered, for 1½ hours, stirring occasionally. Cool thoroughly; transfer to covered storage container. Store in refrigerator for up to 2 months. Makes 3 cups.

PUMPKIN MARMALADE BREAD

2¼ cups all-purpose flour
¾ cup packed brown sugar
¾ cup granulated sugar
4½ teaspoons pumpkin pie spice
2¼ teaspoons baking powder
¾ teaspoon ground cinnamon
¼ teaspoon salt

1¼ cups LIBBY'S Solid Pack Pumpkin
4 eggs
½ cup (1 stick) butter or margarine, melted
⅓ cup orange marmalade
3 tablespoons orange liqueur or orange juice
Marmalade Glaze (recipe follows)

Combine flour, brown sugar, granulated sugar, pumpkin pie spice, baking powder, cinnamon and salt in medium bowl. Beat pumpkin, eggs, butter, marmalade and liqueur in a large mixer bowl until blended. Gradually beat in flour mixture.

Spread batter into greased 9 x 5-inch loaf pan. Bake in preheated 350°F. oven for 65 to 70 minutes or until wooden pick inserted in center comes out clean. Cool in pan for 10 minutes; remove to wire rack to cool completely. Spread with Marmalade Glaze. Makes 1 loaf.

FOR MARMALADE GLAZE: Mix 2 tablespoons orange marmalade and 1 tablespoon orange liqueur or orange juice in small bowl.

Pictured on page 77.

25% lower in fat OLD-FASHIONED NUT LOAF

2 cups all-purpose flour	½ cup packed brown sugar
2 teaspoons baking powder	½ cup CARNATION Evaporated Skimmed Milk
2 teaspoons pumpkin pie spice	1 egg
1 teaspoon salt	1 egg white
½ teaspoon baking soda	1 tablespoon vegetable oil
1½ cups LIBBY'S Solid Pack Pumpkin	¼ cup chopped nuts
½ cup granulated sugar	

Combine flour, baking powder, pumpkin pie spice, salt and baking soda in medium bowl. Combine pumpkin, granulated sugar, brown sugar, evaporated skimmed milk, egg, egg white and vegetable oil in large bowl. Stir in flour mixture until just moistened. Spread batter into greased 9 x 5-inch loaf pan. Sprinkle with nuts.

Bake in preheated 350°F. oven for 60 to 65 minutes or until wooden pick inserted in center comes out clean. Cool in pan for 10 minutes. Remove to wire rack to cool completely. Makes 1 loaf (16 slices). Per slice: 2.5 grams fat and 150 calories.

Pictured on page 77.

ICED NUT AND PUMPKIN LOAF

1¾ cups all-purpose flour
½ cup pecans, finely chopped or ground
2¼ teaspoons pumpkin pie spice
1 teaspoon baking soda
½ teaspoon salt

1 cup (2 sticks) butter or margarine, softened
¾ cup granulated sugar
½ cup packed brown sugar
3 eggs
1 cup LIBBY'S Solid Pack Pumpkin
Icing (recipe follows)

Combine flour, pecans, pumpkin pie spice, baking soda and salt in medium bowl. Beat butter, granulated sugar and brown sugar in large mixer bowl until creamy. Beat in eggs until light and fluffy. Gradually beat in pumpkin and flour mixture.

Pour into greased and floured 9 x 5-inch loaf pan. Bake in preheated 325°F. oven for 1 hour and 15 minutes or until wooden pick inserted in center comes out clean. Cool in pan on wire rack for 10 minutes; remove to wire rack to cool completely.

Spread Icing over top of loaf, allowing some to drizzle down sides.* Makes 1 loaf.

FOR ICING: Combine 1¼ cups sifted powdered sugar and 3 to 4 teaspoons water in small bowl.

*Note: To make design, place 2 tablespoons Icing in small heavy-duty plastic bag. Tint with 1 drop maple flavoring or vanilla extract; knead until blended. Cut a small hole in corner of bag; squeeze to drizzle over loaf in crisscross design.

*Top to bottom: Old-Fashioned Nut Loaf
(see recipe, page 75), Iced Nut and Pumpkin Loaf
and Pumpkin Marmalade Bread (see recipe, page 74)*

Nutty Pumpkin Waffles

2 cups all-purpose flour
¼ cup granulated sugar
1 tablespoon cornstarch
2 teaspoons baking powder
2 teaspoons ground cinnamon
½ teaspoon salt
¼ teaspoon ground ginger
¼ teaspoon ground nutmeg

1¾ cups milk
½ cup LIBBY'S Solid Pack Pumpkin
2 eggs, separated
2 tablespoons butter or margarine, melted
¾ cup chopped nuts
Pumpkin Maple Sauce (recipe follows)
Chopped nuts (optional)

Combine flour, sugar, cornstarch, baking powder, cinnamon, salt, ginger and nutmeg in large bowl. Combine milk, pumpkin and egg yolks in medium bowl; mix well. Add to flour mixture. Stir in butter. Beat egg whites in small mixer bowl on high speed until soft peaks form. Gently fold into pumpkin mixture.

Preheat waffle iron according to manufacturer's directions. Depending on size of waffle iron, pour ½ cup to 1½ cups batter onto hot iron. Generously sprinkle with nuts. Cook for 4 to 5 minutes or until steaming stops. Repeat with remaining batter and nuts. Serve with Pumpkin Maple Sauce. Sprinkle with additional nuts. Makes eight 7-inch waffles.

For Pumpkin Maple Sauce: Heat 1 cup maple syrup, ¾ cup LIBBY'S Solid Pack Pumpkin and ¼ teaspoon ground cinnamon in small saucepan until warm.

Nutty Pumpkin Waffles

Pumpkin Oatmeal Muffins

1½ cups all-purpose flour
½ cup quick or old-fashioned oats
½ cup chopped walnuts
2 teaspoons baking powder
2 teaspoons pumpkin pie spice
½ teaspoon baking soda
½ teaspoon salt

1 cup LIBBY'S Solid Pack Pumpkin
2 eggs
½ cup honey
⅓ cup apple juice
¼ cup vegetable oil
2 tablespoons quick or old-fashioned oats

Combine flour, ½ cup oats, walnuts, baking powder, pumpkin pie spice, baking soda and salt in large bowl.

Combine pumpkin, eggs, honey, apple juice and vegetable oil in medium bowl. Add to flour mixture; stir just until blended. Spoon into 12 greased or paper-lined muffin cups. Sprinkle with 2 tablespoons oats.

Bake in preheated 375°F. oven for 23 to 27 minutes or until wooden pick inserted in center comes out clean. Remove muffins to wire rack; cool slightly. Serve warm. Makes 1 dozen muffins.

Pumpkin Nut Mini Loaves

3¼ cups all-purpose flour

¾ cup quick or old-fashioned oats

2 teaspoons baking soda

1½ teaspoons pumpkin pie spice

½ teaspoon baking powder

½ teaspoon salt

1¾ cups (15- or 16-ounce can) LIBBY'S Solid Pack Pumpkin

1½ cups granulated sugar

1½ cups packed brown sugar

3 eggs

½ cup water

½ cup vegetable oil

½ cup CARNATION Evaporated Milk

1 cup chopped DIAMOND Walnuts

Combine flour, oats, baking soda, pumpkin pie spice, baking powder and salt in large bowl. Beat pumpkin, granulated sugar, brown sugar, eggs, water, vegetable oil and evaporated milk in large mixer bowl on medium speed until combined. Gradually beat flour mixture into pumpkin mixture on low speed; stir in walnuts. Spread into 6 greased 5⅝ x 3¼-inch mini loaf pans.*

Bake in preheated 350°F. oven for 40 to 45 minutes or until wooden pick inserted in center comes out clean. Cool in pans on wire racks for 10 minutes. Remove to racks to cool completely. Makes 6 loaves.

*Note: To make regular-size loaves, prepare recipe and spread batter into 2 greased 9 x 5-inch loaf pans. Bake in preheated 350°F. oven for 65 to 70 minutes or until wooden pick inserted in center comes out clean. Cool as above. Makes 2 loaves.

GOLDEN HERB ROLLS

⅔ cup milk
½ cup (1 stick) butter or margarine
¼ cup water
4 cups all-purpose flour, *divided*
⅓ cup granulated sugar
1 package quick-rising yeast
2 teaspoons dried savory leaves, crushed

1 teaspoon salt
¾ teaspoon dried thyme leaves, crushed
½ teaspoon dried dill weed, crushed
1 cup LIBBY'S Solid Pack Pumpkin
4 eggs, *divided*
2 tablespoons sesame seeds

Combine milk, butter and water in small saucepan; heat until butter is melted. If necessary, cool to 120°F. to 130°F. Combine 3 *cups* flour, sugar, yeast, savory, salt, thyme and dill in large mixer bowl. Add milk mixture and pumpkin; beat for 2 minutes. Stir in 3 eggs and *remaining* flour.

Cover; let rise in warm, draft-free place for 10 minutes or until doubled. Spoon into 20 to 24 well-greased muffin cups, filling ½ to ¾ full. Cover; let rise in warm, draft-free place for 30 to 40 minutes or until doubled. Beat *remaining* egg and brush on top of rolls; sprinkle with sesame seeds.

Bake in preheated 350°F. oven for 30 to 40 minutes or until golden and rolls sound hollow when tapped. Remove from pans; serve warm, or cool on wire rack. Makes 20 to 24 rolls.

Golden Herb Rolls

BAKE-IT-EASY TREATS

When your heart's set on Home-Baked Goodness but you're short on time, Libby's can help. Each of these quick-fixing recipes relies on convenience products, such as Libby's Pumpkin Pie Mix. With such tasty results, a little bit of time in the kitchen will spread a whole lot of pleasure.

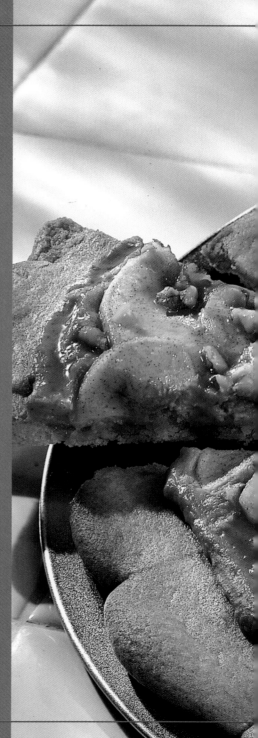

Pumpkin Apple Dessert Pizza
(see recipe, page 86)

Pumpkin Apple Dessert Pizza

1 roll (20 ounces) refrigerated sugar cookie dough
1 cup LIBBY'S Solid Pack Pumpkin
1 package (3 ounces) cream cheese, softened
3 tablespoons granulated sugar, *divided*
½ teaspoon ground cinnamon

1 medium green apple, peeled and thinly sliced (about 1 cup)
Dash ground cinnamon
⅓ cup chopped walnuts
1 to 2 tablespoons caramel-flavored ice-cream topping

Freeze cookie dough for 30 minutes; slice into ¼-inch-thick pieces (about 32). Place slices, edges touching, on greased 12-inch pizza pan.* Bake in preheated 350°F. oven for 12 to 15 minutes or until golden brown. Remove from oven; prick with fork. Cool on wire rack.

Beat pumpkin, cream cheese, 2 *tablespoons* sugar and ½ teaspoon cinnamon in small mixer bowl until smooth. Spread over pizza crust to within ¾ inch of edge. Mix apple slices with *remaining* sugar and dash cinnamon in small bowl; place on pizza. Sprinkle with walnuts.

Bake at 350°F. for 8 minutes more. Place on wire rack. Drizzle with caramel topping. Cool slightly. Cut into wedges; serve warm. Makes 12 servings.

*Note: Recipe also may be made in 13 x 9-inch baking pan. Bake crust in preheated 350°F. oven for 15 to 17 minutes or until golden brown. Add apple topping and bake for 10 minutes more.

Pictured on pages 84 and 85.

Pumpkin Pecan Bread Pudding

½ loaf Italian or French bread, cut into ¾-inch cubes (about 5 cups)
1¾ cups (15- or 16-ounce can) LIBBY'S Solid Pack Pumpkin, *divided*
1½ cups (12 fluid-ounce can) CARNATION Evaporated Milk
3 eggs
½ cup packed brown sugar
½ cup coarsely chopped pecans
1 teaspoon vanilla extract
¾ teaspoon ground cinnamon
¼ teaspoon ground nutmeg
  Pumpkin Caramel Sauce (recipe follows)

Place bread in greased 8-inch square baking pan. Combine *1 cup* pumpkin, evaporated milk, eggs, brown sugar, pecans, vanilla, cinnamon and nutmeg in medium bowl. Pour over bread; press bread into egg mixture. Place square pan into 13 x 9-inch baking pan; fill outer pan with hot water to 1-inch depth. Bake in preheated 350°F. oven for 45 to 50 minutes or until set. Serve with Pumpkin Caramel Sauce. Makes 6 servings.

FOR PUMPKIN CARAMEL SAUCE: Combine ½ cup caramel- or butterscotch-flavored ice-cream topping, *remaining* pumpkin and ¼ teaspoon ground cinnamon in medium saucepan. Warm over low heat, stirring frequently. *Do not allow mixture to boil.*

Easy Pumpkin Ice Cream

2 quarts vanilla ice cream, softened
3¼ cups (30-ounce can) LIBBY'S Pumpkin Pie Mix

Combine ice cream and pumpkin pie mix in large bowl; mix until blended. Pour into ice-cream maker; freeze according to manufacturer's directions.* Makes about 2 quarts.

*Note: To make in home freezer, place mixture in large mixer bowl; cover and freeze for 2 hours. Beat with mixer or in food processor until smooth. Cover; freeze 2 hours more or until firm.

PUMPKIN ORANGE POPPY SEED CAKE

25% lower in fat

1 package (18¼ ounces) yellow cake mix
1¼ cups LIBBY'S Solid Pack Pumpkin
⅔ cup orange juice
3 eggs

¼ cup poppy seeds
Orange Glaze (recipe follows)
Low-fat frozen yogurt (optional)

Combine cake mix, pumpkin, orange juice and eggs in large mixer bowl; beat on low speed for 30 seconds. Beat on medium speed for 2 minutes. Add poppy seeds; mix until blended. Spread batter into greased and floured 12-cup fluted tube pan.

Bake in preheated 350°F. oven for 35 to 40 minutes or until wooden pick inserted in cake comes out clean. Cool in pan on wire rack for 10 minutes. Invert onto wire rack to cool completely. Frost top of cake with Orange Glaze. Serve with frozen yogurt, if desired. Makes 24 servings. Per serving: 4 grams fat and 140 calories.

FOR ORANGE GLAZE: Combine 1½ cups sifted powdered sugar and 2 to 3 tablespoons orange juice in small bowl until smooth.

ADD PUMPKIN, CUT THE FAT

- Add flavor and minimize the fat in packaged muffin and cake mixes! Simply replace the oil called for in the package directions with an equal amount of pumpkin. The result is a moist and delicious cake or muffin with less fat.

- Adding pumpkin to mixes in place of the fat also results in a wonderfully moist texture. To taste for yourself, try the Pumpkin Orange Poppy Seed Cake. Because the pumpkin keeps it moist, this cake tastes every bit as good the second day!

Pumpkin Orange Poppy Seed Cake

Pumpkin Crunch Cake

1 package (18¼ ounces) yellow cake mix, *divided*
1⅔ cups LIBBY'S Pumpkin Pie Mix
2 eggs
2 teaspoons pumpkin pie spice

⅓ cup flaked coconut
¼ cup chopped nuts
3 tablespoons butter or margarine, softened

Combine *3 cups* dry cake mix, pumpkin pie mix, eggs and pumpkin pie spice in large mixer bowl until moistened. Beat on medium speed for 2 minutes. Spread batter into greased 13 x 9-inch baking pan.

Combine *remaining* dry cake mix, coconut and nuts in small bowl; cut in butter with pastry blender or 2 knives until crumbly. Sprinkle mixture over batter.

Bake in preheated 350°F. oven for 30 to 35 minutes or until wooden pick inserted in center comes out clean. Cool in pan on wire rack. Makes 20 servings.

Pumpkin Oatmeal Spice Tortes

1¾ cups (15- or 16-ounce can) LIBBY'S Solid Pack
    Pumpkin
¾ cup packed brown sugar
1½ teaspoons ground cinnamon

1 package (18¼ ounces) spice cake mix
2 eggs
½ cup (1 stick) butter or margarine, softened
    Oatmeal Topping (recipe follows)

Combine pumpkin, brown sugar and cinnamon in medium bowl.

Combine cake mix, eggs and butter in large mixer bowl; beat on low speed until blended (batter will be stiff). Spread into 2 greased 9-inch round cake pans.

Bake in preheated 350°F. oven for 15 minutes; remove from oven. Spread with pumpkin mixture; sprinkle with Oatmeal Topping. Return to oven; bake for 15 minutes more. Cool in pans on wire racks. Makes 12 servings.

FOR OATMEAL TOPPING: Combine 1 cup quick or old-fashioned oats, ¾ cup packed brown sugar, ½ cup chopped walnuts, ¼ cup melted butter or margarine and 1 teaspoon ground cinnamon.

 Pumpkin Meringue Tarts

MERINGUE TARTS

 3 egg whites
½ teaspoon cream of tartar
¼ teaspoon salt
¾ cup granulated sugar
   Ground cinnamon (optional)

FILLING

1 package (4-serving size) instant sugar-free
   vanilla pudding
1½ cups low-fat or nonfat milk
1 cup LIBBY'S Solid Pack Pumpkin
1 teaspoon ground cinnamon

FOR MERINGUE TARTS: Beat egg whites, cream of tartar and salt in small mixer bowl on high speed until soft peaks form. Gradually add sugar, beating on high speed until stiff peaks form. Spoon mixture onto lightly greased baking sheets (or use pastry bag with star tip), forming eight round or oval 4-inch "nests."

Bake in preheated 300°F. oven for 30 to 35 minutes or until crisp. Cool on baking sheets for 5 minutes; remove to wire racks to cool completely. Sprinkle lightly with ground cinnamon, if desired.

FOR FILLING: Beat pudding and milk according to package directions; chill for 5 minutes. Add pumpkin and 1 teaspoon cinnamon; mix well. Chill for 10 minutes. Spoon filling (or use pastry bag with star tip) into meringue tarts. Serve immediately. Makes 8 tarts. Per tart: 1 gram fat and 140 calories.

Pumpkin Meringue Tarts

Baking Basics

Measuring Tips

Not all ingredients are measured the same way, so keep this measuring guide handy when baking:

Measuring spoons are different from the ones you use for eating. Generally, these spoons come in a set that includes 1-tablespoon, 1-teaspoon, ½-teaspoon and ¼-teaspoon sizes. Use measuring spoons to measure small amounts of both liquid and dry ingredients.

When measuring liquids of ¼ cup or larger, use a standard glass or clear plastic liquid measuring cup. Place the cup on a level surface; bend down so your eye is level with the marking you wish to read. Fill the cup up to the marking. Do not lift the cup off the counter to your eye while measuring; your hand is not as steady as the countertop.

When measuring dry ingredients, use a dry measuring cup that is the exact capacity you wish to measure. These individual cups usually come in sets, including 1-cup, ½-cup, ⅓-cup and ¼-cup sizes. Using a spoon, lightly pile the ingredient into the cup. Then, using a metal spatula, level off the measure. Never pack dry ingredients except brown sugar. Pack brown sugar into the cup just enough that it holds the shape of the measuring cup when inverted.

Is sifting necessary? Today's all-purpose flour is no longer lumpy and compact like the flour of yesteryear. That's why simply stirring it before measuring is now sufficient. Stirring works well for most other flours also, *except* cake flour, which has a very soft texture and tends to pack down in shipping. We recommend that you do sift cake flour to remove any lumps and to lighten it before measuring.

A dash is a measure of less than ⅛ teaspoon. To get a dash, just add a quick shake or a sprinkle of the ingredient. When a dash is used, it's usually for flavor, and the actual amount is up to you.

Mixing Equipment, Bakeware, and Oven Temperature

When baking, use these tips when considering mixing equipment, bakeware and oven temperature:

Consider a portable electric mixer (hand-held mixer) for light jobs and short mixing periods. For heavy-duty jobs and long mixing periods, use a freestanding electric mixer.

The material bakeware is made from—aluminum, tin, stainless steel, black steel or pottery—and the finish it has, influence the quality of baked products. Shiny bakeware reflects heat, making the browning process slower., while dark bakeware and bakeware with a dull finish absorb more heat, increasing browning of baked goods.

When monitoring oven temperature, use an oven thermometer. Since temperature variances of up to 25° are quite common, it's a good idea to check the internal temperature of your oven before baking. If the temperature is too high or low, adjust the settings accordingly.

Preheating the oven will give you the best results when making baked goods. *All recipe timings in this cookbook are based on a preheated oven.*

If the appearance or texture of a baked product does not seem correct, review the oven manufacturer's instructions for the proper procedure in preheating your oven. Also, after preheating your oven, double-check the oven's internal temperature with an oven thermometer.

Continued on page 96

Libby's